C. E. M. JOAD

THE FUTURE OF MORALS

OTHER BOOKS BY C. E. M. JOAD
PUBLISHED AND IN PREPARATION BY
JOHN WESTHOUSE
49 Chancery Lane London

The Bookmark
The Meaning of Life
Opinions (2 volumes)

PRINTED BY H.O. LOESCHER LTD.
175 REGENT STREET W1

THE FUTURE OF

MORALS

This is a new edition of a book, which, originally published by Messrs. Kegan Paul in 1924 under the title *Thrasymachus*, was subsequently republished in 1936 under the title *The Future of Morals*, with a new chapter covering developments during the period between 1924 and 1936. A further chapter, *Nineteen Forty-five and What Now?* has been written for the present edition, bringing the discussion down to contemporary events.

C. E. M. JOAD, *Hampstead*, JULY, 1945

Published by
JOHN WESTHOUSE
London
1946

THE FUTURE OF MORALS

CONTENTS

CHAPTER I

MORALITY AS THE INTEREST OF THE STRONGER

THRASYMACHUS appears in the first book of Plato's *Republic,* in which the speakers discuss the nature of Justice. Several tentative definitions of Justice are given, which Socrates has no difficulty in showing to be inadequate by the peculiarly irritating methods of dialectic, for which the Athenians so excusably poisoned him. Thrasymachus then breaks in. He is a blustering, overbearing personage, who makes long speeches instead of answering Socrates' questions, and, when driven into a corner, charges the latter rather irrelevantly with having a bad cold and omitting to use his handkerchief.

Required to sustain an unpopular thesis, he is not unnaturally represented as an offensive person. The trick is an old one and argues well for Plato's sense of dramatic fitness. It should not, however, blind us to the possibility of Thrasymachus' position. Justice he says, and by justice he means social morality, is " the interest of the stronger." Asked how he maintains this view, he points out that the stronger control the government and make the laws. These laws are not unnaturally made in their own interest; in other words, matters are so contrived that, by the mere process of obeying the laws, citizens are led to further the interests of those who govern them. Morality, which is the name we give to law-abiding conduct, is, therefore, a device on the part of rulers to ensure subservience and contentment on the part of their subjects. Since subservient subjects are a joy and a credit to intelligent rulers, we may say that justice, which may stand for morality in general, is the interest of the stronger.

The view that morality is unnatural to human beings and is imposed by law in the teeth of primitive instincts which are fundamentally non-moral, recurs at pretty regular intervals throughout the recorded history of what passes for human thought. It rests upon what is called the social contract theory of society, and leads to the conclusion that human nature is fundamentally wicked.

The life of man in a state of nature was, as the philosopher Hobbes tells us, " solitary, poor, nasty, brutish and short." His hand was against his fellows and every man's hand was against him. Men acted offensively[1] towards each other as and when they pleased, and were restrained by nothing but fear for their

---

[1] The term " acting offensively " in this connection is used to cover primitive conduct of the kind which is supposed to attract wicked and violent men, as, for example, carrying off your neighbour's wife, raping his daughter, stealing his spoons, bashing in or otherwise mutilating his face, and so forth.

own safety. Finding this state of affairs intolerable, men agreed to renounce their natural right to act offensively towards their fellows on condition that their fellows made a similar concession as regards themselves. The best thing of all, of course, was to do what you liked to others without their having the right to retaliate. Since this seemed impracticable, the next best thing was to renounce the full liberty to do what one liked, seeing that it was attended by the obviously unpleasant consequence to oneself of a similar liberty in others, and to venture only upon those actions that the law allowed. Society, then, was a *pis aller*. Your neighbour, it was true, could not harm you, but then no longer could you work your own sweet will upon your neighbour. Men lived at peace with one another, not because they were naturally peaceable and law-abiding, but because they feared the consequences of being found out if they were not. Once that fear of consequences was removed, they would revert to their primitive, natural wickedness. Let a man, for example, learn how to become invisible at will and, as Plato points out, no virgin would be safe, no strong-box unrifled. Man, then, is made moral by law; he is not moral by nature.

Now the man who makes the laws is in one sense like the man who has learnt how to become invisible. I do not mean that he can break the laws with impunity, but he can see to it that he has no incentive to break them. Thus we have the majestic impartiality of the modern law which forbids rich and poor alike to sleep in doorways. He can also, as Thrasymachus points out, ensure that, so long as others keep them, his own power will be automatically safeguarded. And, since the law is at once the prop and the mirror of the public opinion of the community, and, since the public opinion of the community is in matters of conduct at once the guardian and the arbiter of conventional morality, we may further say that the habit of acting in a way of which the public opinion of the community approves will be found to conduce to the maintenance of the *status quo*, and hence to the interests of those whom the *status quo* suits.

In the early eighteenth century Bernard Mandeville revived and elaborated the doctrine of Thrasymachus. Society was devised by skilful politicians for their own advantage. This they hoped chiefly to secure by the spread of what was called morality. Addressing themselves, therefore, to men's pride, they pointed out that man had always considered himself to be superior to the brute beasts. Yet, if he indulged his passions as soon as he conceived them, and gave way alike to sensual desire and violent rage, wherein did his superiority consist? Clearly in order to demonstrate their superiority men must learn to master their appetites and restrain their passions. The plain man listened to the words of the flatterer, and, aspiring to live the higher life, transformed himself from a savage into a clerk. The process is known as civilization.

Tamed by his own conceit, man was now fit to live

in society. As a social animal he regarded as virtuous every action on the part of others by which the society to which he belonged was benefited, and stigmatized as vicious the indulgence of private appetites irrespective of the public good.

But the skilful politicians who had planned the thing from the beginning, had taken good care to ensure that the good of society should be identical with their own advantage. Uncivilized man is ungovernable man, but man tamed and tractable, with the bees of social virtue and social service buzzing in his citizen's bonnet, is at once the prop and the dupe of unscrupulous governments. "From which," as Mandeville says, "it is evident that the first rudiments of morality, broached by skilful politicians to make men useful to each other as well as tractable, were chiefly contrived that the ambitious might reap the more benefit from, and govern vast numbers of them with the greater ease and security."

To those who object that morality was invented by God and not by politicians, and that the sanctions of right conduct are derived not from social utility but from divine ordinance, it should be observed that God Himself is the most potent instrument yet devised for securing the performance of conduct beneficial to " the stronger." This at least is true of the great bulk of the gods who have figured in history. On this point perhaps it would be best to let " the stronger " speak for themselves. Napoleon may be taken as a suitable representative.

"What is it," he writes, " that makes the poor man

think it quite natural that there are fires in my parlour while he is dying of cold? That I have ten coats in my wardrobe while he goes naked? That at each of my meals enough is served to feed his family for a week? It is simply religion which tells him that in another life I shall be only his equal, and that he actually has more chances of being happy there than I. Yes, we must see to it that the floors of the churches are open to all, and that it does not cost the poor man much to have prayers said on his tomb." Thenceforward, though an avowed free-thinker, Napoleon set his face sternly against anti-Christian and anti-clerical legislation.

The moral is sufficiently obvious. Men whose lives are miserable and oppressed will either rise in revolt against their misery and servitude, or console themselves with the prospect of generous compensation hereafter. If steps are taken to ensure that their faith is sufficiently lively, they will look to the next world to supply them with the divine equivalents of the champagne and cigars they are missing in this one, an expectation which confers obvious advantages upon those whom it enables to monopolize the champagne and cigars. Tack on the further belief that riches and power in this world are the best guarantees of torment and anguish in the next, and the utility of religion to "the stronger" is sufficiently manifest. The parable of the needle's eye and the story of Lazarus have been responsible for a political and social quietism among the many, which do credit to the political acumen of the early governing class realist who slipped them into the text of the New Testament; and whenever that quietism has showed signs of giving way, a religious revival or the endowment of a church has usually been found the most effective method of dealing with the situation.

" In 1818 one Englishman out of seven being at that time a pauper, Parliament voted a million of public money for the construction of churches to preach submission to the higher powers. In the debates in the House of Lords, Lord Liverpool took occasion to lay stress on the social importance of guiding by this means the opinions of the masses who were for the first time beginning to receive education."[1] God, it seems, is cheaper than a living wage, and no less effective as a means of securing social contentment.

To its superior utility in this respect we must in part attribute the success of Christianity. Of all religions known to man it lays the greatest stress upon those virtues whose practice is advantageous to the stronger. It glorifies weakness and sentimentalizes over failure; its heaven is for the submissive and the inefficient; its hell for the dominant and the proud. Just as the charitable worker takes the revolutionary edge off poverty by distributing coal and blankets to the victims of acute industrial distress, so the priest promotes submissiveness by inculcating the duties of sobriety, meekness, unselfishness, honesty and contentment. These virtues make good workmen and

[1] *The Town Labourer*, by J. L. and Barbara Hammond.

prosperous employers, and, if they are only developed to a sufficient degree, will enable their fortunate possessors cheerfully to put up with bad wages, long hours, wretched houses and social servitude. The contrary virtues of manliness, self-reliance and independence springing from a spirit passionately resentful of injustice, quick to resist an injury and idealistically determined to make a better place of this world, instead of waiting passively for the next one, are discouraged as savouring of pride and self-sufficiency, and as showing a reprehensible tendency to look for help to oneself instead of to God, our help and refuge in time of trouble. The rich, to be sure, possess these virtues; but then the message of religion is *from*, not *to*, the rich.

But Thrasymachus has yet one more observation to make to us before we leave him to turn to the future. The penalty of law-breaking on a small scale is prison, and of trivial wickedness, social ostracism. But what of law-breaking on a large scale, and a wickedness powerful enough to flout the public opinion to which others succumb? These are the qualities of " the stronger " and they reap " the stronger's " reward. The rebel is the patriot who fails, the patriot is the rebel who prevails. This is the lesson of the past, and those who read it may learn that, if only they are strong enough to succeed, they need not trouble themselves about the respectability of their credentials. Nor has the position altered to-day. The man who steals a leg of mutton goes to prison for a month; the captain of industry grown rich on the profits stolen from his workmen gets a knighthood. The man who has murdered the wife who has annoyed him gets hanged for his pains; the man who kills his fellow-men for nourishment is denounced as a cannibal; but the great general who plans the death of vast multitudes of his fellows whom he has never seen, with whom he has never exchanged a cross word and whom he does not require for purposes of sustenance, is hailed as the saviour of his country.

Thus those who commit injustice, but have the wit or the good fortune to escape the consequences of their actions, climb into the seats of " the stronger" and share their immunity from moral restrictions. Since, in the mere process of gratifying their tastes, they are enabled to give employment to large bodies of their fellows, they are accounted public benefactors whose wealth constitutes a social asset. And, should vestiges of the morality of the weaker, from whose ranks they have risen, assail them in the form of conscience, they discover that even the gods can be squared and that a liberal support of deserving charities, coupled with the occasional endowment of a church, are calculated—so they are assured—to procure for them as honoured a place in the hereafter, as their own successful injustice has obtained for them in the present.

Thus Thrasymachus' phrase "morality is the interest of the stronger" has a double significance. In the first place, it defines the morality of the many as that kind of conduct which promotes the interest of the few; in the second, it assures to the successful

few the honourable reputation, the social consideration and the good repute among their fellows, which
are commonly supposed to be the rewards of
morality.

CHAPTER II

HERD MORALITY AND THE NEW TYRANNY OF THOUGHT

THE statement of general principles in the preceding chapter was not undertaken solely for the pleasure of political and ethical speculation. My concern is a more practical one. If the principle that justice is the interest of " the stronger " is the explanation of what passes for morality, what, I wish to ask, is its application in the present and what is it likely to be in the immediate future?

In order to answer these questions we must first consider a further one: Who in a modern community is " the stronger "?

The fact that we are a democracy has not escaped notice. In our own day it is not kings, nobles, soldiers, prelates, politicians, or elected persons who are " the stronger," but the common man, the plain man, the average man, the man in the street, whether city man or working man, and the crowd or herd of such men. He, or rather his female counterpart since she is more numerous even than he is, is the arbiter of morality, and the kind of conduct which is called moral is that which is convenient or pleasing to her.

Plato with his usual acumen foresaw the possibility of this development, and was careful to provide for it within the bounds of Thrasymachus' formula. All that it is necessary to do, if we wish to apply the formula to a democracy, is to invert it; for " stronger " read " weaker," and the formula remains unaltered. The practicability of this inversion is demonstrated by one, Callicles, in the Dialogue called *The Gorgias*. Most men are stupid, irresolute, apathetic, mediocre, timid, and unimaginative. The qualities implied by these epithets, though discernible at all times, force themselves most pressingly upon the attention when men act together. Take a sheep and stand it on its hind legs and its resemblance to a human being is scarcely noticeable; but stand a flock of sheep on their hind legs and, so far as psychology and behaviour go, you have a crowd of men. In other words, taken severally men may be individuals; taken together they are a mere transmitting medium for herd emotion. Their individual stupidities are added together, but their individual wisdoms cancel out.

In a democracy, says Callicles, the common men are the more numerous; they also possess the power. Acting, therefore, in accordance with their natures, they make the laws which their natures demand. Now it is natural for every man to wish to obtain as much as he can. It is also inevitable that in a state of nature the stronger should obtain more than the weaker. Hence the weaker, acting in self-defence, so frame the laws that the endeavour of one individual to obtain more than the many is stigmatized as unjust. Hence justice, or morality, which is now revealed as the interest of the individually weaker but collectively stronger, may be regarded as their device for depriving the stronger of the preponderance of good things, which the stronger's superior talents would naturally procure for them.

What we may call herd morality is, therefore, a form of self-defence dictated partly by fear, and partly by envy. The source of the fear is obvious; the envy springs from the natural spite of inferior persons who are conscious of their inferiority, resent it, and wish to take it out of those who make them feel it. " I have not," says the average man, " the capacity of the strong man for acquiring a large share of the good things of life. Therefore I will take advantage of my numbers to lay it down that such acquisition is wrong and unjust." The common view of self-denial may be taken as an illustration. The average man has neither the courage nor the strength to satisfy his desires and indulge his passions. Being unaccustomed to moderation he thinks that if he permits himself any indulgence, he will be unable to stop. He dare not bend for fear he break. Hence for the Greek virtue of temperance we get the modern praise of self-denial, with a resultant standard of morality which denounces all bodily indulgence as wrong. Upon the basis of this standard of morality the principle of sour grapes proceeds to operate on a large scale. The man who is not rash enough to take sexual pleasure where he finds it, the woman who is not attractive enough to have the opportunity of being rash, combine to denounce the delights at which the

17

independent and the charming are not afraid to grasp.

Herd morality, which is based on fear and envy, is made effective by blame. In modern society the power to blame is chiefly expressed in two ways. First, by the old whose morality consists in blaming the young; secondly, by the average whose censure descends upon the exceptional.

Upon the part played by the old in maintaining morality I do not wish to dwell, since it differs little to-day from what it has always been. A mistake which all societies have made is to entrust the management of their affairs to the old. Old men are naturally more vindictive, bad-tempered, malevolent, and narrow-minded than young ones. They are easily provoked to disapproval, and dislike more things than they like. Having for the most part lived their own lives, they have nothing left to do but to interfere in the lives of others. They form the governments, misrepresent the people whom they oppress, preach to the people whom they exploit, and teach the people whom they deceive. They mete out rewards and punishments, sentence criminals to death, direct businesses, make laws which they have no temptation to disobey and wars in which they do not propose to fight. If the country were handed over exclusively to the governance of men under thirty-five, and everybody over that age were forbidden to interfere on pain of being sent to the lethal chamber, it would be a happier and a better place. Unfortunately the young men are too busy trying to make a living in the subordinate positions to which the old men grudgingly admit them, to have the time or energy to interfere with other people. Besides, being young, they wish to live, a process for which the regulation of the lives of others is a poor substitute.

In the sphere of morality the function of the old is confined to discovering methods of deterring the young from pleasures of which they themselves are no longer capable. Old men give young men good advice, no longer being able to give them bad examples, and old women invent a symbolic Mrs. Grundy to intimidate their daughters into resisting the temptations which now pass them by. The deterrent influences so exercised are called morality, under which name they impose on the young, who will not have caught their elders lying often enough to disbelieve them, until they have begun to produce sons and daughters of their own, by which time they will be only too ready to abet the prevailing hypocrisy.

The other strand in the fabric of modern morality has already been noticed as the tendency of the weaker to get even with the stronger by taking it out of him on moral grounds. Morals, it is thought, are everybody's privilege and everybody's possession. Few of us can understand Einstein's theory of relativity, but we all know the difference between right and wrong. Hence the man who is deficient in talent can make up for it in virtue, and, by assuring himself that God's noblest work is an honest man, put brains and capacity in their proper place.

Since the motives which have prompted its invention

persist unchanged, morality, which has always been the special emanation of the herd, varies little in spite of superficial differences from age to age, whilst intellectuality throws off new lights in every age. There is probably very little difference between the crowds of ancient Babylon and modern Clapham, but the mind of Einstein differs in radical particulars from that of Archimedes.

Realizing that any fool can be good, intellectuals have always made light of morality for the same reasons as those which have caused the herd to set store by it. If the herd has been ready to censure the eccentrics, the eccentrics have been even readier to provide materials for censure. Despising the mob, they flout their standards and laugh at their scruples. The good are so harsh to the clever, the clever so rude to the good, that one might almost be tempted to believe in a fundamental antipathy between virtue and brains. Whether this be so or not, it seems probable that there is some necessity in our natures requiring us to exalt the common qualities we share and understand, and to condemn rare gifts. Thus morality represents the average man's attempt to console himself in the face of the insulting superiority of the few, by proving that the superiority is achieved only at the cost of loss of virtue. Certainly we must take it out of these fellows somehow! It tortures our self-respect to admire those who have qualities we cannot possess. That is why we love to think of the philosopher as an absent-minded fool, incapable of feeding himself, writing cheques or catching trains,

and listen so greedily to the legends of vice and volup-
tuousness in men of genius.

Wickedness in high places is so much more appe-
tizing than wickedness in low; it enables us to prove
that those who are inconsiderate enough to rise above
us in place and power, only do so at the cost of falling
below us in simplicity and virtue. At the time of
writing, the public lips were smacking over the details of a case in which it was alleged that a wife
endeavoured to advance the career of her husband by
a liaison with the Quarter-master General of H.M.
Forces. It was further alleged that the husband con-
doned and even encouraged her conduct. The
Quarter-master General was a man of marked ability.
His organizing and administrative capacity were
justly famous; he was, in fact, one of the few brilliant
successes of the war. When the rumour spread that
this man, one of the most powerful as well as the
ablest in the land, had been willing to advance a
subordinate because he desired his wife, the outburst
of public indignation in the Press was tremendous.
Wickedness in high places was a glorious theme; there
had been nothing like it since the Armistice. Labour
bodies met to insist on the superior purity of the lives
of working people, and parsons thundered in their
pulpits against the luxury of the rich. For several
weeks the " Dennistoun case " was the chief subject
of conversation in trains, buses, and bar-parlours,
and those whose lips smacked the most greedily over
the luscious scandal were the most severe in their
condemnation of the vices of society.

Why was it that this case attracted so much attention? Why was the wickedness involved considered so shocking? Why did those who would not have looked twice at the six-line paragraph describing a similar occurrence in the remoter suburbs follow every detail of the case with the most avid curiosity? Because the woman was unusually beautiful, the man unusually powerful and talented. The beauty of the woman aroused the envy of other women; the power and talents of the man excited the envy of other men.

We all of us have an impulse to blame those whom life has more generously gifted or more fortunately bestowed than ourselves. We make a virtue of our deficiences, argue that only the dull and lowly are good, and call the feeling of envy which we experience for those who are neither dull nor lowly moral indignation.

In addition to the envy of the old for the young and of the herd for the exceptional, the impulse to blame, which men call morality, owns another source. This is the desire for uniformity. The desire for uniformity springs in its turn from the fear of insecurity. Society, says Schopenhauer, is like a collection of hedgehogs driven together for the sake of warmth. The object of social observances is to put felt upon the spikes in order that the proximity of the hedgehogs may not cause them to injure one another. The risk of friction will be reduced to a minimum, if all the hedgehogs behave in the same way. Identical behaviour in all circumstances is, no doubt, an unattainable ideal; but this makes it doubly important that the herd as a whole should know within limits in what way each of its members *will* behave. Those who react unexpectedly to familiar situations, or differ markedly in their conduct from others, are a danger to the herd, causing social friction and a sense of insecurity. For this reason reformers like Christ or Ibsen, who violently question the standards of thought and conduct prevalent in their herds, and refuse to conform to them, are regarded with bitter hostility.

The method by which the herd secures the uniformity of conduct upon which its comfort and security depend is the exercise of social approval and disapproval. In extreme cases this method is forcibly employed. The soldier who shows a tendency to run away under the enemy's fire endangers the safety of his fellows. Steps are accordingly taken to check this tendency by the pressure of social disapproval in the form of discipline. Discipline is a device for substituting the certainty of being shot for those who do not go over the top for the probability of being shot for those who do. The result is that most soldiers go over the top. This is conduct conducive to the safety of the herd, and is rewarded with social approval under the name of courage.

More usually social approval and disapproval find expression in the sphere of manners and modes. In Japan under the old laws the term for a rude man is " other than expected fellow," and a noble is not to be interfered with in cutting down a fellow who has behaved to him in a manner other than is expected

In general, thought or conduct calculated to surprise or disturb the herd incurs disapproval and is called immoral; thought and conduct which mirrors the beliefs and habits of the herd is regarded with approval and is called moral. Thus virtue is the habit of acting in a manner of which other people approve; vice in a manner of which they disapprove.

Summing up, therefore, we may say that social morality in a democracy springs from the envy of the average man for the talents of the able man which cause him to feel inferior, and from the dislike of the herd for the conduct of the eccentric which makes it feel unsafe.

These are general principles and are more or less applicable in any state of society which is not a tyranny or a close oligarchy. What I wish to emphasize is their special application to a modern western democracy.

In a community of this type the herd is at once more congested[1] and more powerful than it has been in any other period of history. Its congestion causes it to place a hitherto unparalleled emphasis upon the necessity for felting the spikes of the hedgehogs, that is to say, upon the importance of uniformity; its power enables it to vent its disapproval upon those who offend its prejudices with the maximum effect. This can be seen most clearly in the case of America which has produced the most congested and the most powerful herd on record. America is a melting-pot

[1] The word "congested" is used to denote the oppression of spiritual stuffiness rather than of physical overcrowding.

in which all the races of the earth are fused. The natural diversity of its elements produces a special need for artificial uniformity in its citizens. A civilization with its roots in the earth can allow its members to spread outwards, like the branches of a tree; a civilization, whose seeds are planted in shallow soil, must hedge them about lest they be scattered by the wind. The first is centrifugal: it can tolerate individuality because it has a centre. The second is centripetal: it must enforce uniformity because it has none.

For this reason all American citizens strive to be exactly like each other, and, on the whole, they succeed. They have the same clothes, they live in the same houses, they have the same social habits, the same respect for money and the same suspicion of such superfluous eccentricities as thought, culture, and art.

A friend of mine who had wintered in a Southern State, as the season advanced discarded his felt hat for the regulation straw. A few weeks later he had occasion to travel northwards to New York. As he left the train he noticed that he was an object of atention to people on the platform. Porters and loungers stared, and as he walked away from the station, he found himself followed by a small and apparently hostile crowd. Hailing a taxi, he drove to his hotel. In the porch he met an acquaintance, told him of the notice he had attracted, and asked the reason. His friend explained the matter by pointing to his straw hat. It was too early in New

York for the change over into straws, he said, and of course one could not dress differently from other people.

The rigid enforcement of uniformity is hostile not only to freedom of action but also to independence of thought. The laws against teaching or holding doctrines displeasing to the majority are particularly severe in America. Immigrants, for example, are not allowed to land in America until they have first expressed their disbelief in Communism, atheism and free love. Many people are put in prison for holding unpopular views, although these views do no apparent harm to anybody. Advocacy of birth control, possession of irreverent and disreputable books, expression of subversive opinions with regard to the relationship of capital and labour, and disbelief in God are among the offences so punished.

Not only is it necessary not to profess unpopular views—it is sometimes necessary to profess popular ones. Indeed, in order to placate herd opinion " the stronger " enforce by law the propagation of deliberate falsehood. This happens especially in those cases, unfortunately only too numerous, in which the truth is less gratifying to human conceit than we could wish, so that its adoption involves the abandonment of cherished beliefs. Such, for instance, is the belief that man is a degenerate angel, which is thought to be more flattering than the truth that he is a promoted ape. Hence the famous repudiation by the State of Tennessee of the " monkey ancestry " of its citizens. A law was passed under which it was illegal for any teacher in a university or other public school to teach anything which denies the story of creation given in the Bible, or to affirm that man has descended from the lower orders of animals. It is not, so far as I know, maintained even in America that the doctrine of evolution is untrue. It is sufficient that it incurs the disapproval of " the stronger." Thus truth herself is liable to be stigmatized as immoral, if she is inconsiderate enough to flout the wishes of respectable citizens.

Where individuality is to a large extent obliterated, and citizens are cut according to approved specification by the social machine, nothing is so much valued as personality. I have said that every American wishes to be like every other American, and so he does—but with a difference. He wants to have a personality of his own. He wishes to have a something about him that will convey an impression of uniqueness and cause him to be talked about among his fellows. Nothing is so much discussed in America as personality. Men try to cultivate it as they try to cultivate biceps; agencies exist in order to tell you how to be unique, and psycho-analysts flourish by the simple process of telling you that you are unique.

But this is just what the conditions upon which herd morality depends will not let you be. Depart one hair's-breadth from the standard habits of thought and accepted codes of conduct, and the herd will make your existence intolerable, until you consent to toe the line.

Now the drift of British development follows increasingly the course set by America. America is our most advanced nation in morals as in everything else, and if we want to know what England will be like to-morrow, we cannot do better than look at America to-day. America is at once a signpost and a stimulus. What American business men are, or rather have been, that do our business men still strive humbly to be. They ape their magnificence, and enjoy a large and increasing share of their power. The stockbroker's conception of the good life is becoming increasingly accepted by the clerk, the clerk's by the shopkeeper, the shopkeeper's by the workman, so that the community as a whole is doing its best to live up to the standard which its business men set. So soon as we have got rid of the last vestiges of our dying aristocracy, such as our respect for hunting and our maintenance of a semi-feudal tenantry, we shall subside into an inferior and imitative satellite of the States.

The objects of American civilization are to substitute cleanliness for beauty, mechanism for men, and hypocrisy for morals. It devotes so much energy to obtaining the means to make life possible, that it has none left to practise the art of living. Hot baths and more hot baths, larger and ever larger hotels, faster and ever faster cars, golf played by ever grosser and more vulgar men, and lap-dogs kept by ever fatter and more vulgar women, cocktails and wise-cracks, psychoanalysis and faith-healing, gangster literature and sensational sport, supported and maintained by an illiterate governing class ready to be imposed upon by any quack or charlatan who can persuade it to take an interest in what it imagines to be its soul, such is the probable development of bourgeois civilization in England.

Hints of the growing adhesion of the herd to the ideals and pursuits of big business are not wanting in current developments of moral sentiment. As the profiteer supplants the aristocrat as the dominant force in the community, a slight twist is given to the moral opinions of the herd as a whole, in order that they may be brought into line with the changed interests of " the stronger." Moral sentiments suitable to the interests of a hereditary aristocracy of landed proprietors insensibly give place to a morality designed to protect and safeguard the pursuits of the fat man on holiday.

An example of this process is afforded by the changed attitude to hunting. A hundred years ago hunting was considered an entirely honourable pursuit, appropriate to gentlemen and advantageous to the countryside. To-day it is attacked on humanitarian grounds and voices are raised in favour of the fox. If he must be killed, why not humanely? Take, for instance, the following. A fox chased by the Cowdray hounds jumped through the window of a private residence and up the chimney-flue. Efforts were made to smoke him out by lighting a fire immediately below, for all the world as if he were a boy chimney-brush of a century ago instead of a fox, but they were unsuccessful. Ultimately workmen removed some bricks and the fox was got out and given to the hounds. The case caused an outcry on the ground that the fox, who had given the hounds a good run, was the victim of cruel and unsporting conduct. A similar outburst was provoked by a hunted stag who recently took refuge in the Channel, and was picked up and carried to France.

That hunting is now condemned by the moral sense of the community not because of any increase in humanitarian sentiment, but because of a change in the interests of the predominant herd, is shown by the apathy of public opinion with regard to the victims of the gun and the motor. Business men, unable to hunt because of the obesity produced by their habits, are not debarred from shooting. Moors are hired in Scotland, and all creatures liable to interfere with the supply of game are ruthlessly exterminated. Thus a squirrel-catching society has been formed in Aberdeenshire. Rewards are offered for each squirrel captured, and it is estimated that between two and three thousand squirrels are killed a year. At Monte Carlo business men sit on terraces and shoot down pigeons which have been previously imprisoned in darkened boxes, with the result that, when they are let out into the sun-light, they are too dazed to fly away. Before they are placed in the boxes the tails of these birds are removed. This impedes their flight and makes things easier for the business men, who kill between sixty and a hundred an hour. But it is not thought, except by cranks, that the business men are immoral for amusing themselves in this way, although it is illegal in England for boys to steal the eggs of many kinds of birds.

In the south of England, where the roads are tarred to facilitate the passage of motors, and the approach of business men is heralded over the countryside by a stink of oil and petrol, it is reported that the emanations from the roads have poisoned the waters of the Test and Itchen and caused the death of many of the living things that dwell in them. Even the fish, it seems, have begun to feel the march of progress.

Business men are given to amassing property, but not to making friends. It is not in personal relationships that they seek the good life, but in a plenitude of goods. For this reason current herd morality visits offences against property with greater severity than offences against the person. A man will get six months for stealing a diamond necklace, but only six days for beating his wife. But, though the ill-treatment of a wife by her husband is punished with comparative lightness, her appropriation by another man is considered to be the height of wickedness. This is because the man who makes love to his neighbour's wife is committing an offence against property. For the same reason the desire on the part of a wife to secede from her existing possessor and to be an independent entity maintaining herself by her own exertions is regarded with disfavour. It is as if a valuable house were to insist that it should remain uninhabited.

Those who belong to a herd are in general unable to understand the wish of others to escape from it. Such

31

a wish is an implied criticism upon the herd conception, and brings a sense of insecurity. Thus the desire for leisure and solitude, or for a life amid wild
surroundings, is regarded with instinctive disapproval. A Frenchman recently exploring in Brazil
came upon a party of Indians, one of whom had a
paler skin than the others. The pale-skinned Indian
turned out to be his long-lost brother, who had lived
among the Indians for a number of years. The explorer immediately set to work to persuade his
brother to return with him to civilization. His efforts,
however, proved unavailing. The brother asked why
he should return to a community in which he had to
pay taxes, wear clothes and do other disagreeable
things, when he could live with the Indians in a state
of nature without labour of any kind. The explorer
had no answer to these questions. He was unable to
understand this refusal to return to the herd and accept the restrictions that existence in the herd involves. Accordingly he told his brother that he was
a hopeless degenerate, and left him to what he
characteristically called " his fate."

Something of the same feeling is entertained by the
average man towards the artist or the writer. He dis-
trusts the contempt of herd standards which his
irregular life implies. This sentiment is reinforced
by a feeling of insecurity in regard to possessions. The
average man is too busy to spare time for sexual immorality, and instinctively suspects the life of the
artist or writer because of the facilities which it affords
for meddling with his wife during office hours. The

general nature of the objection entertained by the herd to sexual immorality will be examined more fully in the next chapter.

Before I close this chapter I wish to point out how the sentiments I have endeavoured to describe have been intensified by the decay of religion.

Communities in which the average man is "the stronger" have always been noted for their Puritanism and high moral standard. Promiscuity has historically been practised by the aristocracy rather than by the middle classes, and in societies in which the standard is set by the latter is visited, accordingly, with a disproportionate amount of moral obloquy. Severer steps would no doubt have been taken against it had it not been for the conviction that the sinner would be punished hereafter. The poor man, lacking the rich man's goods, has comforted himself with the story of Lazarus. But the moral man has found equal consolation when denying himself the pleasures of the flesh, in picturing the eternal torments which awaited those who refused to be bound by his inhibitions.

The average moralist has accordingly refrained from punishing the successful libertine, knowing that God would do it for him. But this conviction is no longer held. God is a much more mysterious being than He used to be, and we have less knowledge of His ways. It may be that He does not exist at all, and in any event the belief that He will do this or that, and, in particular, that He will entertain the same moral views as we do ourselves, is no longer entertained with its old-time certainty. "Vengeance is mine, saith the

Lord, I will repay." Perhaps it is, but it might be visited on the wrong people. In any event it is safer to take no chances, and to make sure that sinners shall suffer in this world the punishment which the eccentricity of God's views may permit them to forgo in the next. For this reason, it is to be expected that the herd morality of the future will develop a severer outlook upon derelictions from the standards of behaviour which it regards as moral. What these derelictions are, and what are the reasons for supposing that in spite of this attitude they are likely to increase, I will consider in the next chapter.

CHAPTER III

THE NEW LIBERTY OF ACTION

IMPORTANT forces are, however, at work in the contrary direction. If the growing prevalence of herd morality will tend to place a new emphasis on the importance of uniformity, uniformity in the moral sphere is likely to prove more difficult of attainment.

Two factors in particular will militate against it. These are the growth of economic independence among women, and the practice of birth control. Let us consider these factors separately.

I. The basis of the institution of marriage is economic. Theological factors have, of course, played their part. The early Christian fathers, expecting the immediate end of the world, saw no reason to take steps to ensure the continuance of the race. The Christian hostility to the pleasures of the senses was, therefore, allowed to rage unchecked, and sexual intercourse was denounced as both wicked and unnecessary. As time passed, however, it was found that the world showed no signs of coming to an end, an inconsiderateness which led to the necessity for a change of attitude. The Church met the situation with a complete volte-face. It had previously stigmatised the sexual passions as so wicked that no Christian should be permitted to indulge them; it now pronounced them to be so sacred that no Christian should be permitted to indulge them without the sanction of the Church. The sanction of the Church was given in marriage, a device whereby the Fathers sought to control and to regulate the workings of a passion they were unable to ignore. Since then the Church has claimed both the ability and the right to sanctify sex, and has looked with disfavour upon marriages consummated by the State as an infringement of her monopoly.

But the fact that marriage has been instituted by God and cornered by the Church is not sufficient to account for its existence before the Christian epoch or its stability since. These rest upon an economic foundation.

Throughout the recorded history of civilisation the only recognised way for a woman to make her living has been through her body. Her body being her one saleable asset, she could employ it in either of two ways. She could sell the use of it to one man for an indefinite period, or she could lease it to a number of men for short and strictly regulated periods. The first method is known as marriage; the second as prostitution. The existence of these two, and of only these two, ways of gaining an economic livelihood has led to the formation of two unofficial women's Trade Unions, the Trade Union of wives and the Trade Union of prostitutes. The strength of these unions is directly proportional to their monopoly of the economic field, and far exceeds that of any recognised

Union in the more strictly industrial sphere.

It is immediately obvious that any woman who was prepared to give for love or for nothing what other women were only prepared to give for maintenance, was a blackleg of the most subversive type, and the whole force of organised female opinion has, therefore, been devoted to making her position impossible. The force of female opinion so directed is known as morality, and the bitterness with which the free lover, that is to say, the woman who loves outside the marriage tie or the prostitutes' preserves, is denounced as immoral, is due to women's unconscious recognition of the fact that she is cutting at the basis of the economic livelihood of their sex.

It is, of course, true that the two women's Unions are to some extent competitive, and that the existence of the prostitute threatens the security of the wife, while it guarantees the chastity of the young girl. For this reason there is and always will be hostility between the Unions. The wife's first commandment is the Deity's " Thou shalt have none other woman but me," and she is accordingly accustomed to regard the prostitute with horror, whereas she does not object to the existence of other wives, since this does not, at least in theory, threaten her own. For this reason, too, the method of earning a living adopted by the wife is generally preferred to that adopted by the prostitute, and is esteemed the more honourable by public opinion. So true is this that in most women the belief in the honourableness of wifehood has become second nature, the really nice woman feeling instinctively that the only decent way for her to live is on the earnings of some man. But while this feeling provokes hostility to members of the other Union, it is a hostility which cannot compare in bitterness with the scorn and hatred felt for the free lover. The reason for this is obvious. The number of women a man can have for money is limited by the extent of his income; the number of women he can have for nothing is limited only by the extent of his ability to find them. For this reason it is felt instinctively that the free lover is a greater menace to society than the prostitute. The prostitute, indeed, is and always has been recognised as a social necessity. She guarantees the chastity of nice women by providing a necessary solace for men up to the comparatively late age at which modern economic conditions allow them to marry. Thus in Tsarist Russia the brothel was a State recognised institution. A new brothel was formally opened by the police officer, and was hallowed by a religious ceremony in the course of which the premises were blessed by a Russian Orthodox priest.[1]

Sexual morality in men springs from the same economic source, but is more limited in scope and less fiercely embraced. This is a natural deduction from what has just been said. If the livelihood of women is bound up with the strict observance of the marriage tie, the maintenance of the moral restrictions upon which marriage as an institution depends is their special concern. In a purely promiscuous community

[1] *Report of Labour Delegation*, 1925.

the livelihood of women would be intolerably insecure. Hence women are the natural guardians of morality, knowing that it guarantees their bread and butter. It is not too much to say that morality as a going concern is kept up by women. Men on the whole, despite their strong property sense, are not interested in moral questions. They have not the woman's delight in nosing out scandals and, except when they are whipped up into a state of moral horror by their womenfolk, are much too prone to live and let live. The attitude of deliberate uncharitableness towards erring sisters which the sex affects, does not come naturally to men, and, left to themselves, they would condone offences which their outraged spouses insist on punishing with social ostracism.

It is on the whole true to say that the moral sense, so far as sex is concerned, only begins to function in men after marriage and, except in the case of one's own daughter whose saleable value in the marriage market is thought to be diminished by inchastity, it centres upon the wife. Since the wife is in origin a piece of property purchased by the husband for his own enjoyment, to her must be extended the jealous guardianship which presides over property in general. The wife is the most valuable of a man's indoor possessions; in return for the use of her body he has agreed to maintain her in such dignity and leisure as he can afford. This obligation to maintain the wife is a permanent one, persisting even after the enjoyment of her person has ceased. Thus when a wife divorces or lives apart from her husband, he is usually required to maintain her, so long as she remains chaste. So soon, however, as she bestows the enjoyment of her person upon another, the obligation to maintenance ceases, presumably on the ground that the new consumer should be saddled with the obligation of keeping up what he enjoys. In nothing is the property basis of marriage more clearly discernible than in the " dum casta " clause of the English divorce law.

It is upon the same economic basis that the husband's objection to infidelity chiefly rests. If another man is permitted to enjoy for nothing what he himself has purchased at a heavy outlay, the husband naturally feels aggrieved. He is also rendered ridiculous. It is for this reason that the cuckold is always presented in literature as a comic figure; he is in the position of a man who is unconsciously having his pocket picked. The husband's predilection for fidelity in the wife is thus as strong as the wife's demand for fidelity in the husband—at times it is even stronger—and springs from the same economic source. So long as the wife is in essence a piece of property, it is naturally felt that only the man who has paid for her should have the use of her; so long as a woman can only obtain her living by selling herself to a man, she not unnaturally demands that others should not be allowed to under-cut her.

I have spoken of this situation, as if it existed in the present; but it is already in many respects an affair of the past. The history of the last fifty years has recorded the growing and continuous influx of women into wage-earning employment which bears no relationship to sex. Women cure the sick, plead in the law courts, teach in the schools, do manual labour in garden, field, factory and workshop, and serve increasingly as clerks, typists and shop assistants. Three were recently found among the five hundred applicants for the post of public executioner in Hungary.

Men have not unnaturally resented this change. The dependence of women has on the whole suited them, and they do not like to see those whose economic helplessness has made them a natural prey to male predatoriness rendered capable of standing on their own feet. Having deliberately deprived women of the skill, the training, the knowledge and the qualifications necessary to make their way in the world, men have then proceeded to justify themselves by proving the moral and intellectual inferiority of women from the fact that they are ignorant, unskilled and uneducated. When it is remembered that the same causes that have left woman no alternative but concubinage (married or unmarried) or starvation have compelled her, as often as not, to perform the duties of an unpaid housekeeper, it is not difficult to see how much man was the gainer by the transaction. But, unfortunately for him, he has been unable to stem the rising tide of feminism. It has long ceased to be true that a woman's only means of earning her living is by exploiting her sex attraction, and all the evidence points to the fact that the number of women in wage-earning employment will be augmented in the future.[1] This estimate leaves out of account the possibility of the endowment of motherhood, which will place all mothers, whether married or unmarried, in the category of independent wage-earners.

The effect of this economic change upon the situation I have briefly sketched, and upon the moral sentiments to which it gives rise is likely to be twofold.

In the first place, the unmarried woman will tend increasingly to form temporary, irregular unions. This result will follow:

(1) Because her knowledge that she can earn her living in other ways will not force her to demand from the man a pledge of life-long maintenance as the price of her love.

(2) Because knowing that she is not dependent upon a man for her livelihood, she will no longer have the incentive to pander to the man's demand for virginity in his prospective wife by remaining chaste until marriage.

(3) Because a man's abandonment of the connection which she has formed with him, a process commonly known as desertion, will not as heretofore leave her stranded without means of support.

(4) Because men will be less chary of forming temporary, sexual relationships with women, when they know that they are not expected to keep them.

In the second place, the married women will tend to mitigate her hostility to irregular unions formed by unmarried women when she realizes:

(1) That her husband's mistress, not being dependent upon him for support, will constitute a less formid-

---

[1] This was written in 1925. As I have explained in Ch. V, written ten years later, the evidence is now all the other way.

able threat to her own livelihood.

(2) That the possible transference of her husband's affections and consequent withdrawal of financial support will not leave her necessarily incapable of finding other employment.

(3) That, as the clear-cut line of demarcation between married and unmarried unions becomes obscured by the increase in the number of the latter, it will no longer be either possible or necessary to put the unmarried mistress as completely beyond the pale of decent society as has been customary in the past.

From the above considerations it will be seen that the growing economic independence of women is likely, unless counteracted by other forces, to lead to a relaxation of the marriage tie, to an increase in irregular unions, and to a growing tendency to dispense with marriage altogether.

But, some critics will object, what about the children? Hitherto I have left the children outside the scope of the argument, and it is high time to bring them in. This leads me to a consideration of the second of the two factors which I cited at the beginning of the chapter, the practice of birth control.

II. That the practice of birth control is likely to increase there can, I think, be no reasonable doubt. I am aware that there is considerable opposition to birth control at the moment, and that various arguments are brought forward to discourage people from employing its methods. These arguments are not held on rational grounds, but are dictated by prejudices based on certain religious or political opinions which those who put them forward profess. It is said, for example, that birth control is displeasing to the Almighty, who invented sexual intercourse for the production not of pleasure but of children; and it is thought, though not said, that it is injurious to the State because it will diminish the supply of cannon fodder and cheap labour.

As regards the Almighty, whether He would agree with the views put forward by those who speak in His name is not known. Until, therefore, we can obtain a direct expression of His opinion on the matter, it is more prudent to assume that His attitude is non-committal, than to supply the place of knowledge by converting our conjectures into dogmas. As regards the supply of cannon fodder, this is supposed to be important for consumption in future wars. Thus Mussolini has recently demanded 1,000,000 more Italian babies. Since, however, those who oppose birth control on the ground that it will diminish the number of recruits, also hold that wars are inevitable owing to the pressure of expanding populations, it would seem that populations which cease to expand have no need to maintain large armies to protect them from the results of expansion.

The position of those who oppose birth control being based on political and religious feelings of an emotional character is not, however, refutable by argument, or assailable by reason. Our business is not to reply to arguments which have no rational basis, but to estimate what influence they are likely to have in the future.

There is, I think, little doubt that this influence will be a diminishing one. Much of the opposition to birth control is little more than an expression of the generalized feeling of hostility which people experience in regard to anything that is new. Whether it be a new morality, a new sonata form, a new way of wearing the hair, a new nail-colouring, a new kind of corset (or none at all), or a new saviour of mankind with which he is presented, man's natural and instinctive reaction is one of antagonism. The antagonism is provoked not by any intrinsic demerit in the thing that arouses it—indeed, in fifty or a hundred years' time it is embraced with acclamation as the last word in orthodoxy or good form—but simply by its newness. The suggestion that any way of life, of thought or of conduct can be better than that which they have hitherto followed wounds people's self-respect, and some time must elapse before they can overlook the offence.

This kind of objection applies in a marked degree to birth control which challenges people's most intimate habits, and seems likely to effect a revolution in their conduct. It will, however, diminish as the idea of birth control becomes familiar. The reaction of the normal Englishman to that which is new usually passes through three phases. He says first "It is absurd," second "It is contrary to Scripture," and third "Of course! I knew it all the time."

There is a further reason for the probable weakening of the anti-birth-control movement. The organized opposition to birth control comes very largely from members of the upper and middle classes. These on an average have very much smaller families than the lower classes in whose interests they profess to oppose birth control, and to whom they denounce it. The inevitable inference from this fact cannot continue indefinitely to remain undrawn, and, as soon as it is drawn, the lower classes will be able to gauge the sincerity of those who exhort them to choose between continence and children, while being themselves remarkable for neither.

Finally, the knowledge of the use of contraceptives is bound in course of time to percolate through every social stratum. The advantages of birth control to the individual are so obvious that few will refuse to avail themselves of the knowledge which the State, in the persons of the medical officers in charge of municipal clinics and welfare centres, at present withholds; while the disadvantages to the community of a system under which the lower strata proliferate unchecked, while the upper and middle classes barely keep up their numbers, will, in the shape of a rapidly deteriorating population, force themselves upon the notice of even the most pious.

Birth control has come to stay; it has also knocked the bottom out of what is called sexual morality.

If the views put forward in the previous chapters be correct, if morality is the interest of " the stronger," and if, where " the stronger " is the herd of average individuals, it expresses itself in disapproval of conduct from which the average, for whatever reason, shrink, then the driving force of morality is to be looked for not in any innate sanction, but in the power which the herd possesses of rendering intolerable the lives of those who flout its prejudices. But in order that the herd may be able to exercise this power, it must be in a position to detect the objects of its censure. This has been possible in the past owing to the unfortunate tendency of sexual irregularity to result in offspring. It is not easy to disguise the existence of a child, and, even if the desperate course of overlaying or otherwise extinguishing it be adopted, the disposal of the corpse presents grave difficulties. Such a course is also open to the objection of doing grave violence to the humaner parental instincts. But birth control precludes the necessity for children, and by so doing makes it possible to " sin " without being found out.

It is not to be expected that people will refuse to avail themselves of the liberty thereby conferred. Whether we are to infer that people are by nature sinful, or simply that a sin which has been manufactured by herd morality is not really a sin, is a question that does not immediately concern us. What does concern us is the impetus which this ability to avoid detection is likely to give to irregular intercourse. Birth control combined with economic independence has brought a new freedom to women. Economic independence enables them to have children, without going either to the altar or into the workhouse. The practice of birth control makes it unnecessary even to have the children.

One further result of birth control may be noticed before we pass on. This is the probable abolition of the double standard of morality for men and women after marriage. That adultery in a wife has always been considered to be more serious than adultery in the husband, the state of the law bears witness. Adultery in a wife is a sufficient cause for divorce; in a husband it[1] must be coupled with cruelty or desertion. This disparity of treatment has always caused grave offence to feminist organizations. Yet the reason for the difference is not far to seek. It arises from the economic dependence of the wife upon the husband. As the result of this dependence, any children which the wife may acquire in the course of her adventures become a charge upon the husband, who is thus required to pay for the fruits of his own shame and another's enjoyment. Where, however, adultery on the part of the wife does not carry with it a risk of children to be maintained by the husband, it becomes an offence neither more nor less serious than adultery on the part of the husband, and the double standard ceases accordingly to operate.

As a result of the above-mentioned considerations, we may expect that the practice of birth control will profoundly modify our sexual habits. It will enable the pleasures of sex to be tasted without its penalties, and it will remove the most formidable deterrent to irregular intercourse.

It is this consideration which lies at the root of the opposition to birth control. Deep down in most of us

---

[1] In July, 1923, the law was amended and adultery in the husband became in certain circumstances a sufficient ground of divorce.

there lurks something of the old Puritanical attitude, which insists that pleasure cannot or should not be had without paying for it. This at least is true of pleasures we do not share. It is this sentiment which is really outraged by the immunity from the consequences of sexual pleasure which birth control confers. Macaulay defined a Puritan as a man who objected to bear-baiting, not so much because of the pain which it gave to the bear, as because of the pleasure which it gave to the spectators. In the same way the great mass of decent middle-class citizens object to birth control, not because of the evil which it does to the race, but because of the pleasure which it gives to those who practise it. The Puritans are up in arms; the dowagers, the aunts, the old maids, the parsons, the town councillors, the social workers, the members of Vigilance Committees and Purity Leagues, all those who are themselves too old to enjoy sex, too unattractive to obtain what they would wish to enjoy, or too respectable to prefer enjoyment to respectability, in a word, the makers of public opinion are outraged in their deepest feelings by the prospect of shameless, harmless and limited pleasure which birth control offers to the young. And if they can stop it, it will be stopped.

Hence concurrently with the increased freedom which economic independence and birth control will give to young people, and to young women in particular, there is likely to be a growth in restrictive and purely inhibitory morality on the part of the middle-aged.

We are in, then, for a wave of Puritanism on the one hand, combined with the possibility of a new liberty of action on the other. What will be the outcome?

CHAPTER IV

THE COMING CLASH

BEFORE I endeavour to answer the question with which I concluded the last chapter, there are one or two additional considerations to which it is necessary to refer, since they must affect our estimate of the future.

I have spoken of the possibility of a new freedom for women, due to birth control and economic independence. Other factors are likely to make such freedom more imperative on social grounds and less intimidating on moral ones.

The first is the preponderance of women in the community. It was estimated in 1921 that in Great Britain there were two million more women than men, and the figures could no doubt be paralleled from other Western European countries. Our existing moral code condemned these two million, and as many more as the number of bachelors entails, to perpetual celibacy and sterility. In other words one woman out of every ten was expected to deny herself the right to motherhood, or to become an outcast from decent society. As the war years recede, the disparity in the numbers of the sexes will no doubt largely disappear, but the enforced celibacy of women due to their numerical preponderance is only one, albeit an extreme, instance of the anomalies which the system of monogamy unmitigated by easy divorce, involves.

This system is intolerable; it is manifestly breaking down in many directions, and it only continues at all because public opinion among women is still too unorganized to protest against it. It is already the subject of wholesale disregard and infringement in practice, and it will be abolished in theory, as soon as the social sense of the community has progressed to the point of removing the stigma from illegitimacy and the reproach from unmarried motherhood. In other words the system is bound up with the man-made convention which insists that the right to have a child shall be saddled with the duty of looking after a man. It seems impossible to resist the conclusion that, where there are not enough men to go round, women will sooner or later be forced in self-defence to permit themselves to have children without husbands.

So far as the right to sexual experience, independently of the right to motherhood, is concerned, this is already safeguarded by birth control. A surplus of women will tend, therefore, through the sheer pressure of virginity, to promote an increase in irregular relationships, and to reinforce the movement towards freedom already described.

Nor will religious considerations deter with their traditional force. I have already spoken of the decline of religious sentiment in connection with the growth of moral vigour on the part of the herd. Lacking the conviction that God will punish wrong-doers, they arrogate the right to themselves. But the same scepticism which lights the fires of the heresy hunters encourages the wickedness of the heretics. If marriages were not made by God, and torment in hell is probably not the result of adultery, there is no longer reason to think that five minutes' bliss must be paid for in terms of eternal damnation. It is, no doubt, true, that God still loves the pure, but when earthly lovers are available, the price of God's love may not be worth the paying. Hence the religious argument, though doubtless it will operate as a brake in a diminishing number of cases, will no longer act as a wholesale deterrent.

A more serious consideration is put forward in the name of biology. " You are," the biologist will point out, " conducting your argument on the basis of certain assumptions with regard to the nature of women, since you predict an increase in sexual irregularity not only among men, but also, and inevitably, among women. Men, it is agreed, are regrettably promiscuous, in the sense that, even if they are monogamous in fact, they are varietist by inclination. But women are different. Their nature is not varietist but monogamous, and it will, in spite of all changes of material circumstances and moral sentiments, remain so. For this reason irregular sexual unions will not increase in the manner you predict."

Biological arguments of this type derived from the alleged nature of women, are in my view mere manmade superstitions. The particular argument in question was invented by the peccant male who wished to convince himself that, however flagrant his own infidelities, his wife would remain faithful, because it was her nature. The superstition was also useful, because it implied that, although a life of unvarying fidelity might do violence to his natural proclivities, he need suffer no qualm of conscience in expecting and exacting conduct which he repudiated for himself from his monogamous wife. The notion too was flattering and appealed readily to male conceit.

Now as to the existence of the fact asserted by my imaginary biologist, there is, I imagine, little doubt. There are, of course, countless exceptions either way, but the general tendency is not obscure. While the cases of My Lord and the barmaid are legion, those of My Lady and the groom are notoriously few. But admitting the fact, are we to regard is as necessarily unalterable? Many, I know, are inclined to do so. Contemplating the domestic tragedies springing from the nomadic tendencies of the male, they have seen in them one more piece of evidence for the satirical plan on which they believe the Universe to have been constructed. If indeed there be design in the scheme of things, to what sort of design do the facts point? To have made man polygamous and woman monogamous they regard as God's most mischievous practical joke, and conclude that whatever may have been the objects and disposition of the Creator of the Universe, they were certainly not those of a gentleman.

But are the facts really unalterable? May they not be the outcome of centuries of servitude and seclusion, made absolute by the knowledge that fidelity meant bread and butter and a home, infidelity starvation or the streets? Since the beginnings of recorded history the great bulk of women have, it is true, remained monogamous; but they may have done so from fear of losing their jobs as wives, if they did not. Those who have been rich enough to stand upon their own financial feet, or powerful enough to snap their fingers at public opinion, have not been remarkable for strict observance of the marriage tie. The cases of Messalina, Catherine the Great, and the modern film star, not to mention a score of less notorious instances, are instructive. Significant too is the frequency of divorce among those who are sufficiently well-to-do to afford the enormous fees exacted by the legal profession from those who wish to change their partners. It is difficult, in the face of evidence of this kind, to avoid the conclusion that the monogamous tendencies of women are the product of training, circumstance and environment, and will not outlast the economic disabilities which produced them.

In any event the present existence of these tendencies, if tendencies they be, affords no indication of what they may become in the future. The fact that the primitive savage could only count on the fingers of one hand does not invalidate the multiplication table, any more than the fact that most women want only one man each now proves that they will not want more in a hundred years. The use of the word " natural " begs the question. We acquire those characteristics which our circumstances and environment demand, and then transmit them to our children in whom, being inherited, they are termed natural. But this does not mean that our children will not in due course develop new characteristics of their own, if a change of circumstances renders the old ones undesirable. There are signs indeed that the new characteristics are already beginning to appear. The attitude of representative up-to-date women on this subject is curious. They tend to deny the difference between males and females which my imaginary biologist alleged, and to declare that their inclinations are naturally as promiscuous as those of their husbands. The circumstance that they control them better argues, they assert, more sense; it does not imply a difference in nature.

Remarks of this kind are often made by women who, nevertheless, live exemplary lives, and would scorn to revenge themselves upon an unfaithful husband by imitating his conduct. Nevertheless, there is no reason to suppose that they deliberately misrepresent their feelings, and we can only conclude that, as usually happens, a new tendency is manifesting itself in thought some time before it is translated into action.

For these reasons, I do not think that any convincing arguments as to the future can be based on the alleged monogamousness of women in the present. Nor, so soon as the force of the monogamous habit wanes, do I think that women will consent to put up with the manifest disadvantages of a system which is based upon the assumption that it is as strong as it ever was. It is certain that they will not be deterred by the protests of outraged males. Conventional morality, as I have already pointed out, like many of our other institutions such as matinées, Wimbledon and the Church, is kept going by women, and directly women withdraw their support, not all the opposition of men will avail to save it.

What then is likely to happen?

Certainly not a relapse into complete promiscuity. The belief that people are fundamentally licentious, and that a partial removal of the barriers with which society has hedged about the business of reproduction, will precipitate the population into a welter of unbridled licence, pleasantly shocking though it is to the minds of respectable people, has absolutely no foundation in fact.

This belief springs from the doctrine of original sin which has always been popular among quiet and well-behaved persons. If man is by nature wicked and sinful, and woman is very little better, then, indeed, contraception and the economic independence of women will lead to an orgy of sex indulgence in which the population will shuffle itself like a pack of cards.

Nothing of the kind is likely to happen.

The purely sexual elements in love have come to occupy an entirely disproportionate amount of attention, owing to the taboos with which they have been vested. Once these taboos are removed, they will revert to their natural position of comparative unimportance. If it were permissible to reproduce the sexual act upon the stage, we should all lose our interest in chorus girls' legs. Moreover, playwrights would not trouble to avail themselves of the permission.

Within reason, continence and constancy are natural to human beings. It is only the intolerable strain to which our absurd social arrangements have subjected them that has caused us to regard ourselves as being by nature unfaithful and incontinent. There is no ground for the belief that the average man or woman who allow themselves to be guided by their own impulses must needs be profligates. For among their impulses must be numbered self-respect, moderation and a sense of what is right and fitting. Because this sense may be, and often is, at variance with the herd morality which is crystalized in the law, it does not follow that it does not exist. On the contrary, it may be in advance of the morality it disowns, so that people, thrown helpless on their passions, may find that honesty, that self-respect, that hatred of cowardice and deceit, and the desire for cleanliness, health and efficiency were master passions, disciplining them far more effectively than the artificial inhibitions of a mediæval morality based on an obsolete religion, and deriving its power from lethargy and fear.

Some changes in social arrangements there will no doubt be. In Russia, for example, where the knowledge of birth control is accessible to all classes, where any two parties by agreement, or either of the two parties by request may obtain a divorce, and where no stigma is placed upon illegitimacy, there has been a considerable relaxation of the family system.[1] If this means, as it probably does, that unhappy families have broken up, and that husbands and wives who disliked each other have availed themselves of the opportunity to make a fresh start, we need not regret the change. Nobody would contend that society is the gainer by condemning the unhappily married to a lifetime of domestic misery, and it is difficult to see why the common sense of the community, which considers the wishes of the parties concerned a sufficient ground for consummating their marriage, does not regard the wishes of the same parties a sufficient reason for terminating it.

On the other hand, it is unlikely that those who are happily married will rush to the Registrar with the object of making themselves miserable by separating, simply because reasonable divorce laws give them the opportunity to do so. It would be an interesting experiment, and one which would enable us to estimate the extent of marital unhappiness, to proclaim a day of conjugal amnesty at recurring intervals. We might, for example, celebrate the coronation of every new king by giving to all married couples the right to dissolve their marriages, and seek other mates. If advantage were not taken of the facilities offered within twenty-four hours, there would be a compulsory reversion to the *status quo ante*. Or it might be better

[1] *Report of Labour Delegation*, 1925. It is interesting to note that this relaxation has taken place concurrently with a marked decrease in prostitution. But see page 85 for a reversal of the tendencies described in the text ten years later.

to fix definite periods between the days of amnesty, so that they would recur at regular intervals. Each general election might serve as a signal for a conjugal, general post, so that couples would have the chance of gaining their freedom every five years. I myself would advocate the institution of such amnesties, although I believe that the amount of conjugal dislocation they would cause would be surprisingly small. It is difficult to avoid feeling sentimental at the prospect of parting even from those whom we dislike, and the fact that couples were no longer bound in law would only tighten the bonds of sentiment. A would feel that, unpleasant as B had been, he could not very well let her down, and B would shrink from leaving A with no one to look after him, even when she had herself looked after him very badly. You cannot, in short, live with anyone for a number of years without dreading the prospect of their loss. The knowledge moreover, that quinquennial escape was possible might lead to married people treating their partners with at least the degree of civility they at present reserve for their acquaintances. I do not think, therefore, that the changes caused by a conjugal amnesty would be very extensive.

For the above reasons, I conclude that the social results of the changes I have been describing would amount to little more than a diminution in the number of unhappy marriages, and an increase in the number of experimental unions.

But it is not to be supposed that the herd will see the matter in this light. Nothing exceeds the licence taken by the imaginations of very rigid people, and there is little doubt that the vast mass of respectable citizens, appalled and horrified by what they will insist on regarding as the prospect of growing and unlimited licence, will rise to meet the situation with panic and persecution. And since, for the reasons already given, morality in a modern community is that kind of conduct which suits " the stronger," we may expect a revival of Puritanism expressing itself in a new robustness and acerbity in the moral sense of the herd.

Symptoms of this revival are not wanting in this country. If, however, we wish to see the clearest portents of what is coming we must, as I have hinted above, look to America. America, as I have already pointed out, leads the world in morals as in everything else. That American citizens set great store by morality is notorious. With their constant Purity Crusades, Puritan pogroms, Vigilance Committees and popular juries of selected citizens, who visit surreptitiously and report upon the moral tone of New York plays, they put our more decadent civilization to shame. On what sort of lines do these engines of American morality take action? One instance must suffice. One, Miss Jewell Barker, recently went bicycling in white knickers. Her outraged neighbours showed their sense of this vicious act by proceeding to seize and flog Miss Barker's father. This is at once to usurp and to invert the divine privilege of visiting the sins of the fathers upon the children.

America is, of course, pre-eminently the Land of

Liberty, and we cannot hope to emulate her highest feats. Evidence is, however, not wanting of our endeavours to live up to the standard our cousins set.

I will quote at random one or two American examples with their British parallels.

America. There is sumptuary legislation designed to check the licence of the stage. " There is," we are told, " a rule in some American towns that the chorus girls must wear stockings, although the principals are allowed to appear with bare legs."

England. There are recurrent protests in the provinces against the indecency and unpleasantness of the plays produced in London. Respectable citizens complain that they never can tell what salacious beastliness may not be sprung upon their protesting eyes and ears, what searchlight cast upon the Augæan stables of high society. Actors and actresses have expressed their views, pointed out that a pure stage is as good a paying proposition as a nasty one, and invoked the case of Gilbert and Sullivan operas to bear witness to the truth of their contention. These operas, a notorious commercial success, have never been known to bring a blush to the most bourgeois cheek. A number of London women have, accordingly, banded themselves together vowing to purify the stage. Protests are to be made nightly in theatres at which plays to which objection is taken are performed. " We shall stick at nothing," said the leader of the campaign, " to make our protest effective."

Concurrently with this development there has arisen a demand for a stricter censorship. It seems not improbable that we are on the threshold of a period resembling the early seventeenth or middle nineteenth centuries, when life as it is will be driven off the stage by the Puritans' demand for life as it ought to be, love will give place to sentiment, and reality to romance.

America. A new teetotal version of the Bible has appeared in America. The festive passages are all dry, the words " raisin cake " taking the place of the word "wine" wherever the latter occurs in the Authorized Version. Thus we read, " And he dealt to everyone of Israel, both men and women, to everyone a roll of bread, a portion of meat and a cake of raisin."

Scotland. Steps were recently taken to transfer to Scotland a film depicting the explorations of Livingstone. An extract from the daily paper tells us that " Prohibitionists there are already strenuously objecting to the incident which shows Livingstone, after he had been found by Stanley, drinking champagne with his rescuer! The difficulty is that the incident is historically correct . . . and the problem is whether truth should be suppressed in the interests of morality. ' At any rate,' said the Secretary of the London Missionary Society, ' the raising of the question *is evidence of the progress made since his time.*' " It can scarcely be doubted that if the meeting had taken place to-day, Livingstone would have acknowledged the march of progress by drinking water.

A straw shows the direction of the wind, and I should not be at all surprised to see Scotland go dry in the next fifty years, especially if she is successful in obtaining Home Rule. If Scotland goes dry, it is not to be expected that England will fail ultimately to follow suit. The increase in efficiency among dry workmen is very great, and if the business men remain " the stronger " in the community, they cannot continue indefinitely to be blind to its advantages, especially as they themselves would be immune from the hardships it entails. If we ask whether an officially dry but unofficially wet business class, and a working class which is dry both officially and unofficially, does not mean one law for the rich and another for the poor, our answer is that conventional morals always does mean this.[1]

The practice of virtue, we are often told, is dependent upon the possession of a sufficient income. It is only the well-to-do who can afford to be generous, honest and unselfish, because they have no temptation to be otherwise. But what is true of virtue is equally true of vice, and the experience of the working of prohibition in America showed how easy it is for the rich to procure illicit indulgences which are out of the reach of the poor.

There is likely to be legislation against wantonness in dress. By wantonness is meant the practice among females of unnecessarily exposing parts of their body. The curious belief that the body is in some way disgraceful, and that the exhibition of it is, therefore, wicked is very prevalent among Western peoples. It

[1] Cp. the case of the legs of the chorus and the principals, p. 62.

arises partly from natural prudery, partly from the property view of marriage, and partly from the inclemency of the climate which makes bathing a comparative rarity.

The conviction that the body is wicked and ought to be concealed is important, because it leads women to expose portions of it which they would otherwise protect, and rightly protect, from the rigours of the atmosphere, in the belief that they are making themselves attractive. Thus women, swathed in layers of furs in respect of the rest of their persons, will venture forth on the coldest day with bare bosoms and open-work stockings. It is with the same object that, though their religion bids them mortify the flesh and refrain from making themselves a stumbling-block to others, they will appear at dinner with necks, bosoms, backs and arms completely naked, a proceeding not only acquiesced in but encouraged by their males. This sort of thing is anathema to the herd, who cannot afford the evening dresses and the furs, and to the old, the condition of whose bodies does not, except in the case of the incurably optimistic, permit them to take the same liberties as their daughters. Hence we may expect a considerable stiffening of public opinion in the matter of decorum in dress and a return to the days in which everything except the hands and the face was carefully covered up.

In the sphere of what is called sexual morality we may expect a growing tendency to make wickedness (that is to say conduct which is not in the interests of " the stronger ") punishable by law. Attempts will be

65

made, and sucessfully made, to multiply crimes by Act of Parliament.

A good example of this tendency will be found in the Bill entitled *The Children, Young Persons, etc., Bill,* introduced by a Labour Member during the tenure of office by the Labour Government of 1924. It represents bourgeois or herd morality in "excelsis." Commonly known as the *Offences against the Person Bill,* its object was to codify and extend the existing enactments against abortion, cruelty to children, offences against children and neglect of children. Many of its provisions were admirable and afforded what is no doubt a necessary protection to children against suffering and neglect. Nevertheless, it menaced individual liberty in two ways. In the first place, it increased the number of offences punishable by law, often in an arbitrary manner. For example, it was made a crime punishable by two years' hard labour for a girl of sixteen to have intercourse with a young man over eighteen, the criminal being not, as one might have expected, the elder of the two parties concerned, but the girl. She alone was liable to imprisonment; the young man was allowed to go free. It was also a criminal offence to conceal the birth of a dead child, to cause or encourage a child to beg, or to celebrate the marriage of a boy and a girl under sixteen, such marriages being declared invalid.

In the second place, the Bill authorized grave interference with personal privacy. The officers and inspectors charged with executing its multifarious provisions were given unlimited powers of search, and authorized in certain cases to arrest without warrant. Even if a Bill of this kind were to be administered by angels or sages, the opportunities for espionage and surveillance which it bestowed would be sufficiently offensive. Since, however, its provisions would in fact be enforced by inspectors and constables drawn from the lower middle classes, who would be only too willing to denounce as flagrant immorality whatever transcended the experience of Clapham, the measure revealed itself as an attempt to endow the herd with increased powers of interference and control over the private lives of those who venture to stand outside it.

Encouragement would also have been given to malevolent and offensive persons who wished to do harm to their neighbours by laying information against them. In general, liberty would be diminished, offences multiplied, and the individual rendered more subservient to public opinion than he has been for a century.

Another expression of herd feeling will be a growing tendency to inquire into the private lives of those who hold public appointments. The herd, that is to say, will increasingly demand of those who fill positions of eminence and authority in the land that they shall conform in practice, and profess to conform in belief, to the list of prejudices and preferences which it pretentiously calls its morals. Even to-day, at the end of a century of individualist thinking, fitness to perform a particular job is one of the least important qualifications in a candidate. What is important is that he shall be a member of a recognized religious sect, such as the Church of England or one of the sub-sects of Nonconformity, that he shall live with one wife. avoid divorcing and being divorced, and display studiously temperate habits. He must also exercise discretion in his public utterances, be judiciously but not violently patriotic in his sentiments, eschew extreme views in politics, refrain from supporting unpopular causes, and on all occasions give the herd the answer it expects. Thus in Wales it is difficult if not impossible for a man to hold any public appointment unless he is a member of a particular chapel, and at English Universities many teaching posts are reserved for those in Holy Orders. Given the capacity for reflecting the opinions and flattering the prejudices of the many, men of acknowledged incompetence may successfully aspire to the most responsible posts. There is, indeed, no post in the country a man cannot hold with credit, if he can only succeed in holding his tongue.

Conformity rather than intelligence is more particularly required of those who seek to instruct the young. A man's ability to demonstrate the differential calculus, or impart the facts of history, would not, it is true, appear to be lessened by his having passed through the divorce court. Yet there is no doubt that such an event will cast a blight upon his career as a teacher. People are too satisfied with their own ways of thought and habits of conduct to wish for their children anything better than that they should think and act as they do themselves. What is demanded of the teacher, therefore, is that he should transmit to the children the same beliefs as those which are held by their parents. He must hold up to their admiration those things which their parents consider to be admirable, such as God, vaccination, monogamy, the Treaty of Versailles and the capitalist system, and speak with scorn and contempt of Bolshevism, atheism, pacifism, free love and agitators, whom parents consider to be evil. When the teacher does this, he is what is called a safe man. He inspires confidence and obtains preferment. Provided, in short, that he guarantees not to teach anything new, his capacity to teach anything at all is not seriously questioned. And, since the best minds of every generation, being in advance of their time, would prefer not to teach at all rather than to perpetuate the dogmas in which they have ceased to believe, the successful teacher is not always remarkable for intelligence.

In any event, whether intelligent or not, he must conform, and will have to do so increasingly. The herd morality which drove a statesman of the calibre of Dilke out of public life because it disapproved of his private life, is, after a temporary relapse, increasing in strength, and in the immediate future nobody who does not profess the morality to which the middle classes adhere, is likely to stand a chance of public office. If a man's actions belie his professions, he must be careful to conceal them.

One of the results of this development will be an increase in hypocrisy. To-day the agnostic don at Oxford worships regularly in the College Chapel, and men will be driven increasingly to give lip service to ideals and shibboleths which in their hearts they despise. In general the gulf which separates public profession and private practice, a gulf which has made England a byword for hypocrisy, will grow wider. Driven to profess the beliefs of shopkeepers, men will rely increasingly upon their private judgment as a sanction for their conduct. Hence the attempt to impose a uniform standard based upon an obsolete morality upon our public men, may lead to a revival of that unfashionable organ the private conscience, and those from whom an unwilling conformity is exacted in public will insist that they and they alone are the judges of what is right and wrong in private.

I have taken the *Offences against the Person Bill* as a typical instance of the kind of legislation in which the new Puritanism may express itself. It indicates a return to the Greek conception that men can be made good by Act of Parliament. In the late nineteenth and early twentieth centuries this conception was regarded with disfavour. As the result of the individualist thinking of the preceding fifty years, the idea that there was one good life which all men ought to lead had been abandoned. The individualist view was that there were different kinds of good lives for different men, as many in fact as there were men to live them, and that it was, therefore, impracticable to establish by law a positive standard of ethical conduct to which all must conform. In so far as law had any function in the matter, it was, by prohibiting violence and the cruder forms of robbery, to guarantee to the community a certain background of order without which no good life was possible. Since the mere process of obeying the law did not make a man a good man, but only restrained him from certain unappetizing kinds of vice by which no decent upper- or middle-class citizen was attracted, it followed that the function of the law was negative merely; its object was to prevent citizens from so conducting themselves that nobody could be virtuous, not to define virtue or to tell men how to attain it. The definition of virtue was a matter for the individual's insight, and the attainment of virtue a matter for the individual's free-will; provided, therefore, that a man abstained from the grosser forms of anti-social conduct which were prohibited by law, the question of what he ought to do and what refrain from doing, was one which he alone could decide.

I believe that this nineteenth and early twentieth century libertarianism in matters of thought and conduct is decreasing and will continue to decrease. The cult of uniformity is hostile to the liberty of the individual, and in order to secure the performance of conduct of which the herd approves, the legislature is likely to assume a more positive control over men's lives than has been customary in the past. We shall, in other words, revert to the conception of one good life for all men, or rather for all poor men, a good life which it is conceived to be the business of the State and of public opinion to promote.

CHAPTER V

NINETEEN THIRTY-SIX AND
WHAT NEXT?

WITH this prophecy I come to the end of what I wrote in 1924 in the first edition of *Thrasymachus*. The rest of the matter contained in that edition, with the exception of one short passage which appears later, has been deleted. In the matter now omitted, I expressed the view that we were " in for " a Puritan revival, but suggested that there can be no real, as opposed to conventional, morality apart from a living religious faith. There was, I pointed out, no living religion in the Western world, and the morality which the preceding pages had analysed and dissected was, therefore, morality only in name, reducible on analysis to the habit of acting in the way of which the majority approved. I have omitted these pages in the present edition not because I disagree with the views they express, but because the events of the last ten years enable me to fill in their outline in greater detail, and to venture a somewhat ampler forecast of the future of morals than then seemed possible. Tendencies, which were latent in the matrix of the times when *Thrasymachus* was written, have in the last ten years come to the surface. Ten years ago everything was in flux. We were at the fag-end of the post-War era and what was to come was obscure. To-day the post-War era has definitely ended and the pre-War era begun, and with the establishment of a new cycle in human affairs there is a crystallization of much which ten years ago was fluid.

I hope that it will not set the reader against me, if I say that this crystallization has adhered with gratifying closeness to the framework whose outlines I dimly discerned in the shifting flux of ten years ago. I ended with a prophecy of a return to Puritanism, of a strengthening of the herd and of the morality of the herd, and of the assumption of new rights and powers by the State over the individual. This, the fact is alas only too obvious, is precisely what has been happening. My anticipation of a stampede back to herd morality erred only in naming the winner in the race. As readers of p. 61 will have noticed, I spotted America as the leader, and prophesied that in matters of morality England would follow with increasing assiduity in America's footsteps. But the Continent of Europe has caught America and far outstripped her, and to witness the outstanding triumphs of the contemporary herd we must turn to Germany, to Italy and to Russia.

This is no place for an attempted evaluation of the prodigious changes which have taken place on the Continent since *Thrasymachus* was written. Attention may, however, be drawn to two or three of their aspects which bear more particularly on the themes of the preceding pages. In the first chapter, I developed the thesis that morality is the "interest of the stronger," and pointed out that the successful doer of injustice on the grand scale makes use of his powers to prescribe the code of morals which will justify his aggression, legalize its results, and whitewash his crimes. The gangster has only to obtain command of public opinion and the administration of the law, in order successfully to represent as the dictates of loyalty, courage, nobility, and love of country the steps by which he obtained it.

"The patriot," I quoted on p. 12, "is the rebel who prevails." I could scarcely then have hoped that the rise of Hitler to power would provide so admirably apposite a commentary upon my thesis.

Hitler's seizure of power was not achieved without a struggle. For years Nazis fought with Communists and Social Democrats, beat up and were beaten, murdered and were murdered in a thousand street brawls. Bands of young men patrolling the streets trying to break one another's heads are not easy subjects for moral evaluation and discrimination. Whether you glorify both sides as fighting for their ideals, or dismiss the moral pretensions of those who are merely trying to take it out of a rival gang, both are equally admirable or deplorable according to your point of view. Nor, I imagine, can there have been a pin to choose in point of savagery and brutality between the Communists who beat and murdered Nazis and the Nazis who beat and murdered Communists.

However, the Nazis won, with the result that Communists have become the wickedest, Nazis the more glorious, of mankind. Nazis who had the misfortune to be killed by Communists are ennobled with post-humous martyrdom, while their Communist rivals are vilified, imprisoned, beaten, tortured and murdered.

"Justice," Goering has admonished the Public Prosecutor and State Attorneys, "Justice and Hitler's will are one and the same thing." Germans of the younger generation concur: "It is the revolution; it is necessary; therefore, it is good" begins an article in a German youth magazine. So apparently does Hitler. Thus in a manifesto issued in 1932 he denounces "*the bloody objectivity*" of Herr von Papen and his fellow judges, because of their condemnation of Nazis indicted for the murder of Communists at Bethuen. "Bloody objectivity" is apparently the Nazis' translation of "respect for evidence." Truth, in fact, like morality, is nothing but the "interest of the stronger."

The more specifically moral aspects of the counter-revolution in Germany provide a further striking exemplification of the development foreshadowed in the immediately preceding pages. Ten years ago I described this development as a puritan revival. To-day a happy phrase of H. G. Wells's, "The revolt of the clumsy lout against civilization," conveys more closely the flavour of contemporary events. Let us examine the content of the phrase.

Looking back to my schooldays, I can remember the contempt with which I, a clever boy not overgood at games, was regarded by the proud and the athletic.

75

Round and about me were eupeptic young men scoring tries at Rugger and bulls at Bisley, carrying bats at cricket, barking out commands on the parade ground, turning grand circles on the horizontal bars, perpetually saving their sides and bringing honour to their houses. They were the gods of their day and their world. How we envied them! How we looked up to them! How we almost adored them! And, as gods will, they patronized or oppressed, according to their moods and natures, obviously inferior creatures like myself.

In God's good time we grew up. With what result? The world, singularly lacking in opportunities for the scoring of tries and the saving of sides, pronounced the deities of my youth a little stupid. They were good fellows, no doubt, but they had failed to pass their examinations and were, therefore, completely without qualifications. Also they were not very quick in the uptake. And so monotonously, obscurely, behind desks and counters they presently drove their uninspired pens for unappreciative employers and a few hundreds a year. Or they travelled, and sold goods to reluctant shopmen. Or they guarded, unhealthily and in solitude, the less salubrious outposts of the Empire. Let those who wish to meditate on their fate read that tragedy of the public school man, J. D. Marstock.[1] Meanwhile the clever little chaps were finding the world more appreciative than the school. Hard-working and intelligent, they presently

[1] This character study of genius will be found in Harold Nicolson's *Some People*.

came to positions of wealth, of prominence and of power. They became K.C.s, bishops, M.P.s, statesmen, men of affairs, heads of businesses, in which latter capacity they were not infrequently the employers of their erstwhile oppressors. And, sensing this reversal of fortune and resenting it, " the clumsy lout " looked forward, unconsciously, perhaps, but none the less intensely, to a world in which brawn once again counted for more than brain, a world in which action mattered more than thought, an exciting world of loyalty and discipline, of leadership and simple faith, a world, above all, in which one took it out of the clever little blighters who were now so unwarrantably on top. How he would make them squirm when he got the chance! Meanwhile he bided his time. His chance, when it came, was afforded by another strand in " the clumsy lout's " revolt, the average man's flat refusal to go on adapting himself.

It looks increasingly as if the movement of progress has been too fast for those, an increasing number, whose minds have been unable to keep step with it. Progress by its very nature involves a strain upon the human mind—the strain of continual adaptation to new conditions, of novel reactions to novel complexities. It demands not only a high and increasingly high level of development, but certain tolerations and restraints—the toleration of ideas, of habits, and of culture that one does not understand, the restraint of one's primitive desire to " hit out " at what one cannot tolerate.

When the process of change goes too fast, it engenders, inevitably, protest and reaction: the protest of those who, resenting their felt inferiority in face of the achievements, the knowledge, the competence and the reputation of the clever, the cultivated and the learned, are unconsciously looking for a chance of " taking it out of " those who make them feel inferior; the reaction which is born of a desire to return to a simpler and more familiar form of society in which discipline and courage are the virtues of the ruled, leadership and confident dogmatism of the rulers. Thus a civilization in which the speed of progress has outstripped the capacity of the average man to keep up with it, is always in danger of slipping back to an earlier level, as a result of his unconscious protest against the strain which it imposes upon him. " We do not understand all this progress: and we do not hold with what little of it we understand. Therefore we are going to stop it, if we can." So runs the unconscious argument, which, whatever the guise of reputable political or sociological dogma in which it happens to clothe itself—the maintenance of old traditions, the return to a simpler mode of life, the preservation of racial purity, the " clean-up " of moral licence or political corruption, or quite shortly, simply, and mysteriously " the salvation of society " —underlies the reactionary movements of the contemporary world.

What is the upshot of this diagnosis? That when you have made every allowance for the history of post-War Germany during the last seventeen years—for the Versailles Treaty, the collapse of the mark, the ruin of the middle class, the slump of 1929, the legions of unemployed—something is still left over demanding explanation, if we are adequately to account for the more bizarre phenomena presented by Nazi Germany. And this something, I am suggesting, is psychological. Germany, in fact, is desperately putting the clock back, because the clock was going too fast for Germans to keep time.

What is the moral, or rather, what is the effect upon morals? In the first place, the clever men are sacked. Nazis indignantly tell us that before their revolution Jews occupied between 70 and 80 per cent. of the higher posts in the universities and the legal and medical professions. There were in Germany 66 million Germans and 560,000 Jews. The inference, in so far as it bears upon one's estimate of comparative intelligences, seems inescapable, but is seldom drawn, at least by Nazis. Envy, springing from the " natural spite of inferior persons who are conscious of their inferiority, resent it and wish to take it out of those who make them feel it "—I must apologize for quoting my own words—has been given *carte blanche,* and the Jews have been hounded out. As for the intellectuals, the novelists and writers, the painters and poets, the philosophers and scientists, the utopiasts and pacifists, their books have been burnt, and the men themselves beaten, tortured, exiled or murdered. Truly " the clumsy lout " has staged his come-back.

But while recognizing and deploring his hatred of

intelligence, his terror of thought, his dislike of individuality, his intolerance of views not his own, his faith in his ability to endear his own by the infliction of gross physical agony upon those who do not share them, while regretting that he should have made dogmatism a virtue and broadmindedness a crime, we must in fairness concede his possession of the virtues which are the obverse of his vices.

What are these? The virtues of pioneers and crusaders, the virtues of loyalty and courage, of unquestioning obedience and simple faith. "The task of the Teachers' Union is to develop the school in the patriotic and National Socialist idea. . . . There must be training to blind obedience to the teacher."[1] "The events of June 30th" (of June 30th, 1934, of all days in the calendar!), says Bishop Dietrich of Berlin, "have opened the eyes of the blind and shown to the world the unique greatness of Adolf Hitler. . . . Hitler has been presented to us by God. Those who do not place themselves at his side are evil-willed and reactionary." In fact, as Goering has so succinctly put it, "blind acknowledgment of the Party's authority is necessary. Anyone who breaks the Party's discipline will be dropped from the Party."

"Tell us what to think and what to do, and we will follow you to the ends of the earth," is, in fact, the watchword of the young Nazi; and, though we may deplore the voluntary imprisonment of the human mind and the surrender to a self-chosen leader of the

[1] Extract from Decree of Bavarian Teachers' Union.

keys of its cell, it would be idle to deny the single-hearted faith which animates these relapsed primitives.

"We greet the Leader each morning and we thank him each night that he has provided us officially with the will to live." The announcement, one of ten commands for workers, embodies a fullness and richness of faith unknown since the Middle Ages.

There is also the virtue, if virtue it be, of asceticism. One of the major European surprises of the last twelve years has been the appeal of discipline and hardship to the generation now reaching maturity. Let a man arise and cry, " I promise you luxury and riches; I will make you powerful and raise you to the seats of the mighty. Follow me "—and only a few Socialists, Jews and intellectuals will hearken. But let him arise and cry, " I promise you hardship and suffering, obscurity and the obloquy of your elders. Follow me for the sake of our Leader, our country and our cause "—and a whole generation flocks to his standard. These, then, are the virtues of the new morality, a morality so whole-heartedly embraced, so strenuously practised, that, in the fierce glare of its white-hot enthusiasms, those of us who are now reaching middle age begin to wear the appearance of survived Regency rakes straying wan and shame-faced into a simpler and purer age.

What is the bearing of these new trends upon sexual morality? Their overt manifestations are sufficiently familiar. In Germany the feminist clock is put back, and women are turned neck and crop out of the positions they have so hardly won. On an earlier page (p. 41) I hazarded the opinion that men have always in their hearts resented the independence which the ability to earn their own living has conferred upon women. Societies of male predominance in which brawn has for the nonce definitely triumphed over brain are societies of female dependence and eclipse. Events in Nazi Germany have amply borne me out. Women must no longer be doctors, lawyers, architects, politicians, accountants; they must not even labour in mill and factory, except when the needs of rapid rearmament demand the services of the gentler sex for the manufacture of munitions. They must revert to the home, look after their husbands, and breed bomb fodder for the next war.

Motherhood, it is announced, is "the natural duty and honour of women," the Church, the kitchen and the nursery their natural sphere. Ten commandments for women have recently been issued by the Nazi Party. They include the obligations of mental and spiritual purity, of constant remembrance of one's Germanic race, of careful scrutiny of the ancestry of prospective husbands—"you do not marry him alone, but all his forefathers"—of prolific breeding. All are such as men would wish to devise for the conduct of women; few such as women would have thought of for themselves. Women in fact are no longer to think for themselves. . . . But, although they may not think, they may fight and in Italy they are now privileged to be trained as soldiers. Women so regarded are unlikely to find life delightful. To

82

be treated alternately as a toy, a drudge and an incubator may satisfy the aspirations of the female peasant or even of the *petite bourgeoise,* but is unlikely to appeal to the educated women, who, in the generation which immediately succeeded the war, grew up in an atmosphere of equalitarian independence. Precisely how the older German women of the educated classes regard this return to the era of the incubating Gothic Madonna, we are not allowed to know. But if, as it seems reasonable to assume, their feelings are in the least like those which women of similar education and attainments in England and America entertain on their behalf, they must be simmering with moral indignation and a sense of burning injustice. Heroes of the Nazi type are always, one suspects, regarded with a certain amused indulgence by women. Little boys *will* play with soldiers, bigger boys *will* play at being soldiers, and the dressing up and posturing and parading, the heroic attitudes and grandiose speeches, are unlikely to impose upon women to the extent to which they have beglamoured their more impressionable males. But when the grown-up children insist on the women not only playing their games, but playing according to their own very one-sided rules, according to which all the more glorious parts are cast for themselves, while the women find themselves relegated to the rôle of everyday Cinderellas who are permitted and expected every now and then to transform themselves into unapproachable Madonnas, their objections may become serious. It would be intriguing if, after all, the Nazis

83

were to fall not because of the opposition of the Catholics, Socialists, Communists or Jews, but because they could not impose upon the women.

The causes of the present situation are no doubt in part economic. Since the slump came, there have not been enough jobs to go round, and it is to some extent inevitable that women should be called upon to retire from the labour market in order to make way for men. But, here again, I doubt whether the economic analysis is exhaustive. The regression to the primitive which I have diagnosed as one of the root causes of the Nazi and Fascist movements, has probably been at least as effective as economic depression in engendering an attitude to women which is the analogue in the sphere of morals of nationalism and dictatorship in that of politics. The position of women in Nazi Germany could be paralleled in a hundred societies, ancient and modern, in which intelligence has been subordinated to muscle and the savage virtues are preferred to the civilized. Fascist movements, if " the clumsy lout " diagnosis is valid, represent the revolt of the average man against the pretensions of his intellectual superior. As I pointed out on a previous page (p. 33), " communities in which the average man is ' the stronger ' have always been noted for their Puritanism. . . ."

Under the régime of the modern Fascist States, women have ceased to exist for themselves; they are here for the benefit of men. As they sustain men's desires, so they must subscribe to their morals.

84

Alternately borne aloft like soap bubbles and jettisoned as lumber, women are required to conform to the specifically male conceptions of female virtue. They must be good housewives, work hard, and breed often. They must be discreet and modest in public, the " less talked of for good or ill among the men " the better, and they must not seek to enter public life, to hold official positions, or, except in special cases, to take up wage-earning employment. Finally, they must defer to their husbands, they must not bestow their affections where they please—for example, if they love non-Aryans they are decorated with placards inscribed " I loved a Jew," their heads are shorn and they are led in public procession through the streets—and they must be faithful to their husbands. In return, they will be loved, housed, fed, and above all things protected; at any cost and against all comers they will be protected. . . .

Even Communist Russia, which began by shocking the world with divorce arrangements so facile that the population could, and at first did, shuffle itself like a pack of cards, has changed its tune as the dictatorship has established itself, and betrays increasingly the characteristic stigmata of herd morality.

Modern Russia to-day represents the apotheosis of the average man. Heaven is the herd, and the insect in the machine is idealized as the god in man. It is not, therefore, surprising to find that Soviet Trade Unions have recently (Summer, 1935) become supervisors of the behaviour of working men towards their wives and children. They also include among their functions the collection of alimony. Russian husbands who have parted from their wives have apparently been remiss in the payment of alimony. Consequently the Soviet has invoked the assistance of the Trade Unions with a view to ensuring regularity. *Trud,* the central organ of the Trade Unions, is now the champion of the cause of family life. " From now on," says one of its manifestos, " our members should be judged by their attitude towards their family and particularly towards their children." Alimony payments awarded by a court are to be recorded in Trade Union books, and collection to be made by deduction from the worker's wages at his place of employment. Evaders of payment lose Trade Union membership and consequently the chance of finding work. Thus the factory becomes the ally of the family and starvation the price of promiscuity.

On pp. 36-37 I pointed out that a woman has traditionally had access only to one method of maintaining herself, that of selling the use of her body to a man and then living on his earnings. On p. 41 I suggested that for the first time in history this traditional method was beginning to be supplemented by others. As women became economically independent, men's hold over them relaxed, and family life of the patriarchal type began to break up. The events which have occurred in Germany and Italy since I wrote have reversed this process. The effects described on pp. 42-43 are diminishing, and women are reverting to the traditional position described on p. 36.

But is it only in Germany and Italy? Are there no equivalent manifestations in our own country? If it be true that there is in the modern world a definite movement of decivilization, if there is any substance in the concept of "the revolting lout," we should expect resultant manifestations not in one country alone but throughout Western Europe. Are there, then, any such manifestations discernible in England? At his point I wish to give myself marks for the following passage, which I quote from the first edition of *Thrasymachus*.

"The history of morals, like that of politics, follows the swing of the pendulum, and some reaction on the part of each generation from the habits of its fathers seems to be inevitable. In so reacting it reverts to those of its fathers' fathers. Thus each generation tends to take the gods of its grandfathers from the shelf upon which its fathers have placed them.

"To-day we are at the beginning of a period of reaction from the licence of the war. The difference between young people of between the ages of eighteen and twenty-four and their predecessors of seven years ago is very marked. The latter were casual, offhand and easy going. They observed little ceremonial in their relationships with each other, smoked, flirted and made love when and where they pleased, married in haste and repented at leisure or dispensed with marriage altogether, and despised rather than revered the aged to whom they were a constant source of horror and amazement. What is perhaps most noticeable about their successors to-day is their improvement in manners. They are chivalrous to women, considerate to the old, maintain a decorum at dances which is positively Victorian, and instead of hastening to establish sexual relations with whomsoever attracts them, have actually gone out of their way to postpone the fruition of their desires by a reintroduction of the rite known as ' engagement.' "

How should we expand the foregoing sketch in the light of the last ten years? We shall notice, in the first place, something in the nature of a religious revival. There has been the rise of Buchmanism; there has been the stampede of intellectuals into the Roman Catholic Church. Furthermore, although the Church itself remains neglected, there is a crowding of young men into religions organizations. The membership of the Y.M.C.A. in a college known to me at London University has doubled during the last four years.

There is, I think, among the young a new respect for authority of all kinds. I find students more inclined to accept without question what their lecturers tell them, less apt to ask questions for themselves. There is also a growing respect for age. If a man is old, he must, it seems, be accounted knowledgeable; therefore, we may as well listen to him. In trains and tubes young men give up their seats to old men; they also give them up to women. The gentleman, in fact, has begun to reappear as a social phenomenon. . . . There is a new simplicity in contemporary culture. The more fashionable highbrow novelists describe in words of one syllable and sentences of half a dozen words the extremer forms of violence and passion. The " tale of the tough guy " is the distinctive tale of the moment, and it is usually as lavish in violence as it is miserly in words.

There is a decline in the art of conversation. People announce convictions, instead of communicating ideas; talkers do not trouble to obtain listeners; listening, indeed, is becoming a dead art. The young in particular are developing a new technique of " not listening," behind which their perfervid convictions, whether Communist, Fascist or Buchmanite, can shelter unscathed by the weapons of argument, unsullied by the breath of reason.

So sheltered, these new creeds of our time breed in their supporters a hitherto unprecedented confidence. Whereas in the preceding period men sometimes sought to know before they ventured to believe, they now supply the place of knowledge by converting their conjectures into dogmas. The dogmas, masquerading as convictions, engender a novel enthusiasm. The " stupids," submerged during the pre-1926 period, are being encouraged by the atmosphere of enthusiasm, simplicity and conviction to " throw their weight about." The unregenerate natural man in all of us is being emboldened to reassert himself, happily and with gusto. He clamours for a larger air force, he fears for the national security, is jealous of the national honour, and may presently discover in himself a dislike of Jews.

Most disturbing to a middle-aged rationalist such as the present writer, convinced of his ignorance in regard to the nature of the universe, the purpose of existence and the destiny of man, is the certainty in regard to questions to which the answer is unknown displayed by the contemporary embracers of the newer creeds. For example, by Buchmanites. I had recently the privilege of spending some two or three weeks in the company of a Buchmanite whose intellectual pretensions were far from contemptible. I had know him first at Oxford where he had had a highly successful academic career culminating in a First in Greats. During his Greats period he had been an exuberant talker, ready and eager in discussion, given to the enumeration of general principles, and able and willing to knock the bottom out of any conventional universe of discourse whether political, social, moral, or religious, that his company happened to be inhabiting; in fact, a typical clever undergraduate of a kind that Oxford has produced to my knowledge any time these thirty years past.

Just after taking his First in Greats he became converted, converted and "changed." The "change," which was not so much moral—he had always been a virtuous man—as intellectual, was cataclysmic. In place of discussion there was now affirmation, in place of questioning, assurance. If now he doubted, he sought for guidance and was made sure. If a moral difficulty presented itself, he prayed for light, and it was solved. Those questions which have left the greatest minds of all ages baffled and uncertain—the nature of reality, the purpose of existence, the right conduct of life—he now answered with a complete assurance. An intelligent man had suddenly transformed himself into a creature capable of holding beliefs with an intolerant dogmatism hitherto observed only in men ignorant of history and untrained in speculation. Like so many of the contemporary young, he has become exceedingly dull. He never, for example, exchanges ideas. For one who *knows,* exchange of ideas is obviously a bad bargain.

The condition of contemporary Europe, for example, is being discussed. Will there be war? Will the dictatorships last? Can the gold *bloc* hold? He has no opinion—not, at least, on the immediate issues raised. The situation is, he affirms, exceedingly simple. It is the inevitable outcome of human nature, or rather of human sins, the sins of impurity, hate, greed, lust and pride. Either human nature will be "changed," and God accepted by all the peoples of all the nations, a consummation which will apparently inaugurate, if it is not identifiable with, an earthly millennium, or this civilization will go down in blood and ruin, as have all its predecessors which have neglected God. This admittedly looks bad; but what he has seen and heard in the recent tour of his Group in Germany, Denmark and Norway makes it reasonably certain that the next six months will witness occurrences of a religious order, bringing with them a new revelation of God, a new scale of moral values and a new purity of conduct, in the light of which the questions which agitate us will have become irrelevant, the problems non-existent. There is, one gathered, about to be vouchsafed a divine communication to the suffering peoples of Europe. . . .

I give this case in detail because it seems to me an extreme, but by no means untypical, example of the developments or retrogressions in the consciousness of numbers of young men belonging to the generation now reaching maturity all over the Continent of Europe.

Gone are the cynicism, the disillusionment, the flippancy of the post-War years. Instead there is a tendency to take once more the gods of our grandfathers from the shelves on which our fathers have placed them—the gods of simplicity and earnestness, of authority and leadership; even, it would seem, of faith. The change can be seen most clearly in the debates of such a body as the Oxford Union, which, if we may judge from the reverberations of the celebrated " Oxford Resolution," at once leads and reflects contemporary student opinion. Five years ago the actual content of a speech at the Oxford Union was comparatively meagre. The epigram reigned supreme. To make a witticism, to point a jest, to coin a *bon mot,* to introduce the calculated patch of purple—these were the objects of the Union orator. Appropriate remarks he would tell you, as he cheerfully ransacked the eighteenth-century wits for his epigrams, were meant to be appropriated: originality was merely skill in concealing origins.

To-day the atmosphere is different. The speeches tend to be uniformly serious; their virtue is sincerity, their defect dullness. Without eloquence or with young men denounce the provisions of the new Unemployment Act, analyse the Government's Housing Policy, or canvass the prospects of the international control of civil aviation.

How does this changed outlook bear upon the position of women?

The feminist movement has, it is clear, come to a dead end. The tide which swept women into offices and the professions has definitely turned and is on the ebb. The women's victory was always something of a Pyrrhic one. In theory the barriers were down, and women were permitted, they were even encouraged, to penetrate where they could. But the world persistently refused to organize itself so as to make way for them. It offered them dull and drudging work, and on the rare occasions when it was the same work as that done by men, it paid them less for doing it. Incidentally it found that they were good at minding machines, especially those operated in the new light industries of the south. Women apparently stand monotony better than men, and one of the main results of the victory of feminism has thus been a transformation of large numbers of the former slaves of the kitchen into the slaves of the machine.

When the depression came, the middle-class women were the first to feel the pinch. The machine-minders remained and so did the typists; but the doors of the higher posts were slowly but ruthlessly closed. To-day the universities are turning out hundreds of highly accomplished young women, linguists and historians, scientists and physicians, whose services contemporary society shows less and less disposition to use.

I have before me the details of the careers of two young women. The first, educated at Roedean, took a scholarship to Girton, worked hard and obtained Second Class Honours in Part II of her Tripos. The second, a brilliant girl from a poor home, ascending to Cambridge on the rungs of a ladder of scholarships, took a First. It is now three years since they " went down." During those three years the parents of the first have lost their money in the depression, and it has become necessary for her to find employment. After two years' fruitless search, she is now paying for lessons in shorthand and typing, in the hope of being subsequently permitted to take down the letters and correct the grammar of a semi-educated business man with half her brains and none of her accomplishments. The second was offered teaching work, but refused it. She had, she felt, no vocation for teaching. She is now serving behind the counter in a big London store. These cases may be extreme, but they are not untypical. Nor do the older women have an easier time. There are, at the time of writing (summer, 1935), 53,000 middle-class women in London who want employment and are unable to obtain it. Clerical positions of all kinds are reported to be closed to women who have passed their twenty-ninth birthday; a saleswoman's life is often finished at 35. Three agencies, an inquirer found, refused to accept applications for employment by women over 25. Of 2,000 women, found in a recent Employment Exchange inquiry to be out of work for more than a year, 60 per cent. were over 35.

And the result? A definite reaction in favour of domesticity, a counter-march into the home under banners inscribed with the slogan, " Better marry and rule a husband and a kitchen, than be at everybody's beck and call in an office! "

Of this changing attitude there are already a number of manifestations. It is, I suggest, no accident that the number of women candidates for Parliament should have declined at each of the last three elections, and that expert political organizers should be reported as announcing (October, 1935): " There is a growing prejudice against women candidates and it is stronger among women electors than among men."

Or consider the significance of the latest fashions. " The themes," I read in a contemporary survey (autumn, 1935), " are definite—Italy renaissant. militarism triumphant and woman the distraction for tired warriors. No more neutrality. Gone are the beige days of sexual *ennui*. These new clothes are screaming scarlet, sonorous green, the flaming blue of an exploding shell, the strange yellow of poison gas." Women's fashions are at once the prop and the mirror of their morals, and a hat no less than a straw may be a pointer to the direction of the wind. For it is time to return to morals.

What, then, of the effect upon women's morals of the change in their status? Here, again, the economic situation only reinforces tendencies whose origin is non-economic. If I am right in diagnosing a return to the primitive as one of the characteristics of the coming age, then the symptoms whose preliminary manifestations I have sought to sketch are likely to grow more pronounced. Women's morals, in fact, will go up, as their skirts come down. Although we shall not proceed to German lengths, we shall show an increasing tendency to patronize the kitchen and to praise the cradle. Even the Church may stage a come-back. A new mythology of sexual purity will arise, and women, thrown back for their livelihood upon the favour of men, will have a new economic incentive to faithfulness. The new Puritanism which I tentatively prophesied ten years ago will, in fact, develop far and fast.

A reinforcing factor will be the continually falling birth rate. In England the year 1940 will see the peak of our population, which thereafter will begin to decline. The decline, given the continuance of present tendencies, will be startlingly rapid. In her book, *The Twilight of Parenthood*, Dr. Enid Charles supplies some instructive statistics. That during the last sixty years the birthrate of the United Kingdom has halved, falling from 34.1 per 1,000 in 1870 to 16.8 in 1930, that in a word the era of expanding population is over—these facts are common knowledge. Few however recognize how rapidly the decline, once started, will proceed. Herein lies the significance of Dr. Charles's book. She points out that in the maintenance of the population girls are the important element. Until the last decade of the nineteenth century, the average number of girls born to a woman during the whole of her child-bearing period in Northern and Western Europe was between 2 and 2.5. By 1926-7 this had fallen to 0.97. On the basis of these figures Dr. Charles claims to show that the net reproduction rate in England and Wales in 1927 was 0.82, and by 1933 had fallen to 0.75. I give the surprising implications of this fact in her own words.

"The net reproduction rate in England and Wales at the present time (1933) is not much higher than 0.75 and the population has practically ceased to increase. If no further change in fertility and mortality rates takes place a stable age composition will eventually be reached. When this point has been reached, the population will be reduced in the proportion 3:4 in each subsequent generation; . . . a population equivalent to that of England and Wales (about 45 millions) at the present time, would be reduced to less than 6 millions, i.e., about half the size of greater London, in about 200 years."

Now it is not to be supposed that the birth-rate will be allowed to decline, or even to remain stationary at its present level, when the effects of stationariness become manifest, without a tremendous fuss. Some of the reasons which make statesmen and other old persons of eminence think a plentiful supply of babies important are given in the preceding chapters. They are likely to produce an intensive propaganda in favour of larger families. Bachelor statesmen will make speeches in favour of fruitfulness, and spinsters will mew for other people's babies. The garage will become the symbol of social wickedness, and the cradle of social virtue. Sexual faithfulness on the part of the married constitutes the most favourable background for the large family, the union of one man and one woman in one family being the best recipe known among the white races for the production of quantities of children. When the husband knows only one wife, the wife only one husband, then offspring are apt to attend upon their knowledge. Thus the so-called needs of the State are likely to combine with the economic situation and the change of moral and cultural outlook, which I have designated by the phrase " the return to the primitive," to inaugurate a return to domesticity and a strengthening of the marriage tie. How far is this combination likely to prevail?

The answer depends on the importance which we attach to the factor upon whose novelty and significance I have laid such stress in the preceding chapters—the new factor of easy contraception. Nothing has happened during the last ten years to suggest that the emphasis which I laid upon the significance of birth control was exaggerated. On the contrary, we are not even yet in a position to gauge its profounder consequences.

That birth control, formerly practised only by the upper and middle classes, is now penetrating all the way down the social scale, that the birth-rate is as a consequence already less than half what it was fifty years ago, that the population will presently begin to decline at the startling rate revealed by Dr. Charles's figures, that the age-average will progressively go up, the old living longer and becoming more numerous in relation to the ever-diminishing supplies of young —these consequences of birth control are by now sufficiently familiar. Others, no less momentous, are less easy to gauge—for example, the ultimate effect upon sexual morality, with which the preceding pages have been largely concerned. Here, however, one fact may help us. When Charles Booth published his *Survey of London Life and Labour* just over forty years ago he estimated that 20 per cent. of the women treated in institutions who were gainfully employed were prostitutes. In the week in which these pages are being written there has appeared Volume IX of the contemporary *New Survey of London Life and Labour,* prepared under the auspices of Sir Herbert Llewellyn Smith. The volume, which deals more particularly with London leisure, gives 3,000 as the estimated figure for London prostitutes to-day. In spite of the economic pressure upon women, prostitution, it seems, is a dying trade. Unless the purity revival goes ever farther and faster than I am suggesting, it will shortly be a dead one.

What is the inference? Not, I think, a decrease in irregular love-making, for which there is no evidence and which seems on general grounds unlikely; but that men are getting for nothing that for which they formerly had to pay. The " profession," in fact, is being killed by the black-legging of the enthusiastic amateur. It has been the argument of the preceding pages that the delights of blacklegging the prostitute have been made possible by two factors: the first, the economic independence of women, which has enabled them to love without exacting maintenance as the price of their love; the second, birth control, which has enabled them to escape its consequences. Of these, the first may, I am suggesting, during the immediate future, operate less strongly. But the second, which is immeasurably the more important, will operate with undiminished strength.

What, then, are the factors which a contemporary treatment of the future of morals must take into account? First, a development of public opinion in the direction of puritan standards, assisted, perhaps, by a religious revival. The regulations against the revelation of the female form upon the stage and elsewhere will be tightened. The penalties for the publication of what is called obscene literature will be intensified. Unless persons in authority discover in time the sexually damping effects of nudism—if we all went naked, one is tempted to think after a sojourn at a nudist camp, the race would die away owing to the cessation of those practices which are necessary to keep it supplied with recruits—the nudist movement may be suppressed, as it has been in Germany. Equalitarianism between the sexes is likely to diminish, and the power exercised by men over women to increase.

On an earlier page (p. 43) I ventured to prophesy a relaxation of the marriage tie as a result of the growing economic independence of women. As this ceases to grow, and begins indeed, to diminish, the process will be reversed. Hence I anticipate a new respect for marriage, supported by propaganda in favour of the family and the home. Meanwhile, a declining birth-rate will put a premium upon child-bearing while a partial way out of the unemployment difficulty may be found in the large-scale elimination of women from paid employment.

All these factors point in the same direction—that of a return to a stricter morality. There is only one factor on the other side—the factor of birth control, a factor whose solitary force may prove more effective than all the cultural and economic factors added together.

The clash of these forces will produce a situation of very great interest, whose outcome it is not possible to predict. For we have no precedents. During the first thirty years of this century, morals have been growing looser, public opinion broader. Thus birth control has hitherto operated in a congenial atmosphere. On the other hand, puritanical epochs in the past have not had to contend against the fact of birth control. The disabling effect of this factor upon Puritanism has been emphasized earlier in the book. If Puritanism is to be effective, it is essential that sexual delinquency should be punishable. But in order that it may be punished, it must first be detected. Detection has been easy in the past because of the physical consequences of irregular sexual intercourse. Once the consequences fail to occur, detection becomes infinitely more difficult. One probable outcome of the clash of forces is, I think, what I was

101

already predicting on pp. 49 and 50, namely, an increase in hypocrisy. Hypocrisy prevails when the pretence of virtue is important and the practice of vice easy. In such circumstances people are apt to combine the solid satisfactions of vice with the smooth appearance of virtue, thus invoking the aid of hypocrisy to make the best of both worlds.

It seems to me most unlikely that anybody will have the courage to end the farce of the English divorce laws. There was a moment just after the war when this might have been done, but the reform has missed the tide, and any changes in the future are likely to tighten rather than to relax. Divorce being refused, the penalties for adultery may very well be increased. If Fascism obtains a hold in England, we may even see women branded and placarded not merely for keeping company with Jews, but for having sexual relations with persons other than their husbands. The sale of contraceptives will probably be made illegal. For negative wickedness, such as the non-production of babies, there cannot, I think, even under the best-regulated Fascism, be a penalty, the causes of such non-production being unfortunately too various. But for positive virtue in the shape of large families there are likely to be prizes; for example, a man's promotion in the State service may depend upon the number of his children, while bachelors and childless married men may be denied advancement altogether. By these and similar devices a puritanical epoch will endeavour to induce women to conform to its moral mythology, and a nationalist State to induce them to breed citizens. Family life, feminine dependence, herd morality, and the practice of the traditional virtues—all these will be encouraged by every device of propaganda, every implement whether of persuasion or of force, which the authoritative governments of the future are able to command. Yet I doubt whether any or all of these inducements and deterrents are likely to succeed in the face of the single fact of safe and simple contraception.

[The years of endurance culminating in the over-throw of Nazi aggression in Europe and the Far East will inevitably leave impressive marks on our existing ways of life and habits of morality. Contemporary moral values are likely to be subject to new and critical enquiry. I have therefore requested Dr. C. E. M. Joad to bring his analysis and discussion of *The Future of Morals* fully up to date by the addition of this new chapter, completed whilst the book was in the press. PUBLISHER.]

CHAPTER VI

NINETEEN FORTY-FIVE AND WHAT NOW?

THIS book has contracted a tendency to pull out a fresh length of itself every ten years, for all the world as if it were a telescope. It was originally written in 1924 to survey the morals of the post-war world[1] and appeared under the unpromising title of *Thrasymachus* in that series of purple-covered little books with bright white labels on their backs which at once mirrored and nourished the intellectual high jinks of the 'twenties.

Bidden to repeat the survey in 1936, I reported and descanted on the moral repercussions of the rise of Fascism and Nazism. Exhorted to a further repeti-

[1] The *first* " post-war world."

tion in 1945, I look out on the wreckage of a world from which the waves of Nazism and Fascism have receded. What, I am asked, do I find and what expect? The difficulty is to distinguish those trends which are the direct outcome of the war from those which are latent in the matrix of our times. The distinction is important since the first may well diminish as the war recedes, the second increase as the peace develops.

I

AFTERMATH OF THE WAR

Loving and the War

Let us take, first, the moral by-products of the war, in 1926 obsessed, as so many of us were, by the rise of Fascism I prophesied an increase in herd morality. The new societies of Germany and Russia represented, I thought, the apotheosis of the average man. Hence, I looked forward to " a strengthening of the herd and of the morality of the herd " and to " the assumption of new rights and powers by the State over the individual." I made a similar prophecy in 1924. So far, it is clear, my guess was all too accurate. But I also argued—it was the theme of the first four chapters of the original *Thrasymachus*—that " communities in which the average man is the ' stronger ' have always been noted for their Puritanism."

On this point the war has proved me wrong, for during the last six years the morality of the average has not been puritanical—not at all. In war-time Puritanism is at a discount; the god of battles is also, inevitably, the god of brothels and there has been more love-making outside the marriage tie during the last five years than at any time within living memory, not excluding the period of the last war. The reasons for this are sufficiently obvious and need not detain us. New boys have in vast numbers been meeting new girls; husbands have been parted from their wives, wives from their husbands. Both have felt lonely and needed consolation; both have taken it. " At one period before I came on leave," writes an officer serving in Burma in February, 1945, " fifty per cent. of the men in the force to which I was attached applied for compassionate leave on the ground of domestic trouble." The phrase " domestic trouble" means simply that the man applying for leave had been informed that his wife was unfaithful. As Lord Elton has put it, " the family was the first and most tragic casualty of the war." It is not surprising in the circumstances to find the Registrar General in his Report for the year 1943 telling us that " the illegitimacy rate among live births was 16 per 1,000 above the average of the preceding five years," while, if no other evidence were available, the appalling increase in the incidence of venereal disease is a sufficient indication of what has been happening. In England these tendencies have been exacerbated by the presence of vast numbers of foreign troops, ranging, vigorous males, the charm of whose address and the audacity of whose concerted attacks upon the defences of English womanhood have put our quieter English methods in the shade. There have been the Americans, the French, the Italians and the Poles; above all there have been the Poles. Who could resist them?

Shocking of the Author

I suppose I am getting old, old enough to begin to cry " sour grapes " at the pleasures I no longer share. At any rate, I confess during these last years to a feeling which honesty compels me to recognize as analogous to what I have known and laughed at in others as moral reprobation; not to put too fine a point upon it, I have been shocked. " These young people," I have said to myself, " how they do ' go on ' —and in public too." Yes, there lies the rub for the sexually ageing man; they " go on " in public, I was brought up to think not only that one's sexual activities were one's private affair, but also that they ought to be conducted in private. In respect of this belief I am, I can now see, old fashioned.

It is a long light summer evening; all over the West End of London, as I write, young people can be seen, not merely picking one another up but man-handling one another, for all the world as if it were dark. Usually the men are of military, the girls below military age. Throughout the war boys and girls, deprived of parental control, either through evacuation or because mother was engaged whole-time or part-time on war work and father was called up together with the elder brother or sister, have grown to maturity with abnormal celerity and unprepossessing precocity. As a consequence, there has been a large increase of juvenile delinquency, of gangsterdom and hooliganism among boys, and of amateur prostitution among young, sometimes among very young, girls. There they go in groups of three or four parading up and down Coventry Street and Piccadilly before the Americans and the rest. The Americans are reputed to like crowds and to be accustomed to doing things in public. In this matter of love-making they have certainly not belied their reputation. Assuredly they have not hidden the light of their loves under bushels. I, as I confess, have been taught that these things should be done in private and I have been properly shocked.

The fact that the young girls are usually half, and the American and Dominion soldiers wholly "tight" has not, from my point of view, improved matters. Drinking, I have been taught, is like love-making in that it should not be done in public, but unlike love-making in that it may and should be done among a number, a small number, of congenial companions. When a man deliberately takes the muzzle off, what may or may not come out of his mouth is a gamble; therefore, if he is wise, he will see to it that only those who wish him well should be present to hear his indiscretions and his confidences. If, in short, you are to make a temporary fool of yourself, you had best do it among other temporary fools who are also friendly fools. Americans do not appear to share these old-fashioned notions. Their conduct in this matter has been noteworthy in three respects: —

(1) A propensity for getting "tight" on so very little; I can only suppose that they are not used to whisky and gin, for our war-time beer could not have intoxicated a baby; (2) an inability when "tight" to retain their liquor. I have never seen so many people

being publicly sick as during the war. The platforms of tube stations seemed to be specially favoured, and it was impossible during the height of the American invasion to go home by tube at night without seeing three or four patches of evil-smelling vomit on most West End platforms. In this sense, at any rate, the Americans left their mark on the country; (3) a willingness to do both in public.

Drink and Morals

I have said little in the preceding pages about drink because its connection with morals was not so plain to me, as it has since become. An incautious public remark of mine to the effect that I proposed to celebrate V-Day by going to church and then getting drunk with a good conscience evoked such a shoal of letters, private and " open," leaflets, pamphlets and articles from tearful temperance men and outraged nonconformists, culminating in a terrific broadside of denunciation from that old campaigner, Isaac Foot, rebuking me for my ignorance of the awful effects of drink, that my eyes have been opened and I have been brought to see the light. Let me, then, hasten to make amends by now making belated confession, (i) that I consider habitual drunkenness to be evil in itself—evil in that it brutalises the spirit and clouds the reason; (ii) that drink—I have witnessed the fact again and again during the war years—assists what is called immoral conduct. It is a lubricant which oils the wheels of the sexual machinery.

Drinking by the Young

Having thus established the relevance of the subject to the original theme of this book and done my best to make my peace with the temperance men, let me proceed to indulge myself in a few observations and suggestions on the great drink question.

I have recently been reading a Mass Observation *Report on Juvenile Drinking,* compiled in 1945 as a result of investigations in four areas, South-West and East London, a south country port and Mass Observation's traditional north country industrial town, Worktown. The Report describes what is in effect a social revolution. For example, in the industrial areas surveyed the proportion of women in pubs was about three times as large as it had been in 1938. In Worktown the proportion of pub goers under the age of twenty-five had risen from 7 per cent. to 40 per cent.; in London, from about 3 per cent. to 18 per cent. Practically no young men under 18 were found in pubs in Central London, the under 18's being almost all girls, usually in company with soldier escorts from the Dominions or U.S.A., with whom they had been to dances. The girls, who drank much less than their escorts, did not, it appears, visit with them the same pubs as those to which they habitually went to in company with their regular " boy friends." In both the London areas intensively studied a certain number of pubs—not typical of the average— were used as places of meeting and negotiation preliminary to subsequent sexual intercourse.

This revolution in habits is, of course, largely due

to the war—the god of battles and of brothels has always, perhaps inevitably, been also the god of brewers—and will in part disappear with the conditions that gave it birth. Some part of it, however, will persist as similar changes, for example, in the length of women's skirts and hair persisted after the last war.

Suggestions

Supposing that, as I do, you regard these tendencies as regrettable, are there any suggestions that you would feel disposed to make for their mitigation? I venture on three:

The first is a simplification of the law. The summary given in the Mass Observation report shows an unnecessary, an almost incredible complication. For example, a child under the age of fourteen may not enter a bar but is not forbidden to enter the lounge of a public house or of a restaurant, which is used, but not predominantly used, for the purpose of serving drinks. A child can enter the buffet of a railway station where snacks are served as well as drinks, even if drinking is the major buffet activity. If he is over five, the child can drink as much alcoholic drink as he likes, provided that he does not do it on licensed premises. Thus, his parents can go to a pub, leave him outside and then bring him beer to drink in the alley-way. Between the ages of 14 and 18 it is not illegal to enter a bar and you can drink there, provided that you drink mineral water; also, between these ages you may sell liquor in public houses, whether intoxicating or not. If you are over 16 but

112

not over 18, you can drink perry, cider or beer in a restaurant or pub provided you eat at the same time, but you cannot drink spirits, even if you eat. If you are under 14 you can go to the jug and bottle department and there purchase bottle liquor to take away with you, provided that the jug and bottle department is not mainly used for drinking in, and so on. What a muddle it all is!

My second suggestion is that instruction should be given in schools in regard to the uses and effects of alcohol. For more than a century teaching of this type has been officially and semi-officially recommended in schools. Nine of the hundred and thirteen pages in the existing Board of Education Handbook, *Suggestions on Education*, are, indeed, devoted to the effects of alcohol, but the information is rarely communicated to the children. Teaching in regard to the effects of alcohol is voluntary and the investigation showed that only four per cent. of a sample lot of children attending London schools had received any instruction at all.

But tidying up the law and giving instruction in the schools will not alter the basic facts of the situation which, in my view, are the results of the disastrous separation we have made between eating and drinking. Where drink is taken normally and regularly with meals, as it is in France, there is no " drink question "; but when it is unobtainable in most restaurants and at most hours in any restaurant, it becomes invested with an atmosphere of glamour shot through with facetiousness and the direct pleasure of drinking is reinforced by the indirect pleasures of pride and guilt. Prior to the war males spent their evenings drinking in pubs where they could not eat and females their afternoons in cafés where they ate but did not drink, or drank only tea, coffee, milk and minerals. Owing to the treating system which both reflects and encourages the moral cowardice of the man who dares not risk the reputation of not being thought a good fellow and a good mixer, men also drink far more than they can afford to pay for. This bears hardly on women who spend lonely evenings at home, while men are squandering the money which ought to have gone to the feeding and perhaps entertainment of their wives and children in demonstrating their heartiness and good fellowship to other men. To bridge the disastrous gulf between eating and drinking is also to heal the barbarous separation of the sexes, which, outside the ranks of Orientals and savages, is I believe peculiar to the Anglo-Saxon races. The provision of establishments at which both food and drink are provided at all hours and where families could gather complete with children for a joint family meal would, I think, go a long way to solve the problem.

Increase of Toughness

But here, I see, I have alighted by inadvertence upon the main theme of this chapter, that of the relation between the sexes proper, not, that is to say, between soldiers and female children in war-time, but between

114

grown-up men and women at all times and especially in the future.

Before I do so, however, I have a word to say on the fulfilment of another of the prophecies contained in the last chapter of the 1936 edition of *Thrasymachus*. My obsession with the rise of Fascism led me there to prophesy that barbarism would grow and civility decline. H. G. Wells had just diagnosed Nazism " as the revolt of the clumsy lout against civilization." Civilization was putting the clock back, toughness was in the ascendant, and I was looking forward to a return to the virtues and the vices of an earlier and more primitive type of society, " the virtues of pioneers and crusaders, the virtues of loyalty and courage, of unquestioning obedience and simple faith," and, I might have added, the correlative vices of stupidity, docility, insensitiveness, brutality and cruelty.

This prophecy has been fulfilled in full measure. The general lowering of the standards of civilized behaviour during the war has been as widespread as it was inevitable. I am not here referring to the major beastlinesses of our time, to the mass slaughter, mutilation and rape of human beings, to the deliberate cruelties of the concentration camp, to the persecution and ruthless elimination of millions for reasons of race, country or creed.

I am concerned only with the effects upon public morals of a period during which for five and a half years the mass slaughter of our fellow human beings by order of the State has been represented as the highest duty of man, while all those studies, disciplines and pursuits which train the mind, elevate the spirit or refine the taste have been at a discount.

The Predicament of the Young

For hundreds of thousands of those who belong to what is now the coming generation, education has been meagre and intermittent. Apart altogether from the interruptions of education due to evacuation, in the psychological atmosphere engendered by the war any and every reason from air-raids to farm work and from " father's leave " to mother's confinement has been put forward and accepted as an excuse for absenteeism from schools. Children have been taught from fifty to sixty to a class and no small part of the teaching they have received has been directed to causing them to admire the very practices which the religion no less than the good sense of civilized communities requires them to condemn. (I suppose, though, that having little or no religion, this generation has at least been spared the recognition of this most glaring of contradictions.) Having been bidden to " Join the Air Force " by R.A.F. posters picturing an aeroplane hovering above the inferno of a blazing town, it is not surprising that many boys should have adopted for their model what they believe to be the ideal military type, that is to say a stupid, hectoring, self-opinionated, *mono-eidic* lout. The resultant lowering in the standard of morals and manners which has hitherto been accepted as the norm for civilized communities is not in the circumstances surprising.

The Growth of Petty Crimes

I am, I repeat, not here concerned with the major horrors of our time which are too well-known to require documentation from me. I cannot, however, resist the temptation to substantiate the generalisations upon which I have just ventured by a few pieces of evidence culled at random of the war's effects in stimulating dishonesty, insensitiveness and callousness. In the year 1943, losses due to the theft of parcels on the L.M.S. Railway amounted to over one million pounds worth of property. An official of the Railway Company's Association asserted that in the same year, 14,500 electric light bulbs a month were broken or stolen from railway carriages, although the bulbs were useless for ordinary circuits. During the year 45,000 window blinds were torn down or slashed, 2,000 leather straps cut down or removed, 13,000 luggage straps torn down and more than 3,500 mirrors slashed or stolen. Fittings or all kinds were wrenched from the walls of carriages and first-aid and A.R.P. appliances stolen. Police court prosecutions for the ill-treatment of children had in 1944 more than doubled since the beginning of the war. (The rise was, in fact, from 1.1 to 2.8 per cent.) By the same year the daily average population of our prisons had increased from 11,086 in 1938 to 12,800, in spite of a great decrease in debtor prisoners. The increase was most marked in the case of women, particularly so in respect of mothers sent to prison for neglecting their children. Baby farmers have thriven. Their practice, according to the secretary of the National Children's Adoption Association, is to get into touch with unmarried women in maternity hospitals, to arrange to meet them on their discharge and then take over the care of the baby. A substantial proportion of these babies are the illegitimate children of women whose husbands are abroad, a particularly sinister fact being the great increase in the number of babies infected with venereal disease.

There is some evidence for a growth of cruelty to animals, though from the nature of the case this is difficult to prove.

The Decline in Civility

What is indubitable is the enormous increase in rudeness and decline in civility in the casual relations of chance acquaintances or of those who are not acquainted at all. In buses, on trains, in shops, in queues, people are worse in temper, less considerate in manner, more pushing, grasping, self-assertive and predatory. The growth of rudeness is in part due to the usurpation by young women of many duties and services formerly performed by men. There they are, on buses, in ticket offices, behind counters and barriers, bossy, disdainful, negligent, shrill and short tempered. Invest a woman with authority and you transform her into a schoolmistress. Whether women were or were not meant for public office is an open question; that they have little or no talent for it is certain.

As I write, the papers are full of complaints about the inconsiderateness of bus conductresses. They won't, it appears, wait for people. With what contemptuous scorn these young women regard old people who are slow in getting on or off, who fumble for their money, who fail to produce the right change or even who venture to ask them a question; how they rate them for smoking in the wrong place, or at the wrong time, for showing the wrong ticket, for committing some minor breach of minor regulations. (The following, which I take from the morning paper, is typical of dozens of cases: " Another London bus conductress was fined at West London yesterday for failing to take reasonable precautions for the safety of her passengers. It was alleged that the conductress, Mrs. Sarah Pockett, Woolston Street, Holborn, rang the bell of her bus in Uxbridge Road when a woman passenger who had helped a child to board the bus still had only one foot on the platform. The bus started, and both the woman and the child fell.") How they glare and snap at you when you ask them for some small service. Or they look through you, as if you were a pane of glass, or down on you as if you were an insect, or they don't look at you at all. Devoid of sympathy, tolerance or patience, they show an equal determination in standing upon the letter of rules and ignoring their spirit.

This, of course, is on the surface. A deeper cause is to be found in the fact that for six years now there

have been too many competitors for the available services, too many in the buses and the trains, too many
in the theatres and the cinemas, too many in the shops
and the streets; altogether too many everywhere.
That the war should have produced shortages was
only to be expected, but the sudden multiplication
of persons has been one of its mysteries. It isn't
merely that there have been more in the country and
fewer in the towns; there have been more *both* in the
country and in the towns, more in the streets, more
in the hotels, more at the shops, more in the houses.
Yet all the time people are clamouring for more
babies, while the great organs of public opinion have
been rumbling with apprehension as if they were the
national bowels over the decline of the birth rate.
And here at last I come to the main theme of this
chapter and turn from the by-products of the war
which may presently diminish to those tendencies
which seem likely to persist and grow, until in their
bearing both upon the relation between the sexes and
upon the supply of children they bid fair profoundly
to modify the structure of our civilization.

II

PROSPECT FOR THE FUTURE

Nothing has occurred since the 1936 chapter of the *Future of Morals*[1] was written to alter my view that the overriding factor in the situation is the decline in the birth-rate and that its overriding cause is the practice of birth control.

The Birth Rate—The Facts

Since 1936 a number of weighty books have been published on the population question, the most important of these being R. M. Titmuss's *Parents' Revolt.*

Some of the relevant facts have already been glanced at in Chapter V in connection with Dr. Enid Charles's *The Twilight of Parenthood*. I have space here for no more than a brief mention of one or two additional items. When the war ended in May, 1945, there were two million fewer children in this country than there were at the end of the first world war. The decline was not due to an increase in the infant mortality rate which has in fact been much lower in this war than in the last, still less has it been due to the effects of enemy action. The reason is the much

---

[1] Chapter V.

lower birth-rate during the two last decades, although there have been many more marriages and a much higher population of married couples.

It is commonly thought that the birth-rate rose during the war. It did in fact rise at one time but rose very slightly, so slightly that, as Mr. Titmuss points out, during the worst year of the last wear, 1917, it was at 17.7 per 1,000, considerably higher than during the best year of the present war, 1943, when it was 16.5 per 1,000. Since 1944[1] it has begun again to decline. For the first three months of 1945 the weekly returns by the Registrar General have reported a birth-rate varying around 17 per 1,000 while Scotland has just[2] announced that its rate for the first quarter of 1945 was the lowest ever recorded.

I quote here a relevant passage from an article by Mr. Titmuss contributed to a book entitled *Rebuilding Family Life in the Post-war World,* published in the spring of 1945. " In 1918 the total number of women in the reproductive age groups, fifteen to fifty years, amounted approximately to 10,500,000, of whom some 4,800,000 belonged to the highly reproductive group of twenty to thirty-five years. It is significant that these women, in the sternest period of the war, produced between them some 663,000 live births.

" These figures should be contrasted with those prevailing to-day. In 1941 the birth-rate touched bottom

[1] Since the above was written the 1944 figures have been announced. They were 17.4.

[2] June, 1945.

at 14.2; it rose to 15.8 in 1942 and still further to 16.5 in 1943. At mid-1939 the number of women in the age groups from fifteen to fifty was 11,464,000, and in the group twenty to thirty-five it was 5,032,000—i.e., distinctly greater than the corresponding figures for 1918 and it may be computed, not materially different from the figures of 1942 to 1943. Yet in 1942, despite this advantage of nearly a million more potential mothers, there were fewer births—i.e., a total of 654,000—than in the worst year of the last war.

" After the last war the birth-rate rose sharply from the hitherto record low level of 17.7 in 1918 to 25.5 in 1920. In that year 958,000 infants were born to approximately the same number of women as in 1918. From this peak, however, the rate subsided rapidly, falling back to 17.8 by 1926 and then declining less steeply to 14.4 (the lowest between wars figure) in 1939."

So much for the general picture. Here are a few illustrative facts taken at random from other articles appearing in the same book. " In a survey of 2,562 Scottish families, Dennis Chapman found that in 48 per cent. of the families there were no children under the age of fourteen at all. In 23 per cent. there was one child, in 16 per cent. two. In only 13 per cent. were there three or more children."[1] According to the report of a Gallup Poll published in the *News Chronicle* in February, 1944, two-fifths of those who

[1] War-time Social Survey, *The Location of Dwellings in Scottish Towns*, by Dennis Chapman.

were asked gave it as their opinion that the ideal family should have only two children or less; two-thirds specified three children or less. Dr. Margaret Hadley Jackson, Medical Officer to the Devon Family Planning Association Clinics, who in the course of her duties has interviewed large numbers of married people, tells us in the book already referred to[1] that very few of those whom she has interviewed " intend to let nature take her course and chance having a baby within a year of marriage." " The more general attitude," she concludes, " in this country seems to be that the right size for a family is in the region of two, that children are not the natural, inevitable and satisfying fruit of married love to be conceived and born as an act of faith but are, on the other hand, a heavy and formidable burden."

Speaking to an audience of social workers in June, 1945, Dr. David Mace, described as an " expert marriage counsellor," gave it as his considered esti-mate that one marriage in ten is childless and " possibly more than that."

The Causes

The causes are scarcely more in dispute than the facts. They are:—(1) The fact that children instead of being financial assets to a family are now a liability, since they must be educated and cannot, therefore, contribute to the family earnings until they are over fourteen. When the School Leaving Age is raised to

[1] *Rebuilding Family Life in the Post-war World.*

sixteen, the strength of this deterrent will be increased.

(2) The employment of women, involving a late marriage age.

(3) A standard of values which regards "keeping up with the Joneses next door" as the main purpose of existence and rightly regarding cradles as militating against the fulfilment of this purpose not unnaturally prefers cars. The whole climate of our times is unfavourable to families. It is a climate in which cars assist, cradles militate against good reputation. To quote Dr. Eliot Slater, Medical Officer for the Maudsley Hospital, Clinical Director of another hospital, and Assistant Psychiatrist of yet another, "the married man with three children cannot live nearly so well on the same income as the childless pair or the bachelor. The whole structure of our society is against the large family. The family with six or more children is looked on with pity rather than respect, and is a subject for jokes. Houses and flats, cars and entertainments and the advertising that sells them are all designed for the family with at most one or two children."

(4) These tendencies have been intensified since the middle of the war by the shortage of houses and the resultant difficulty of finding accommodation for wife and children, a difficulty which grows in proportion to the number of children.

(5) A preference for quality as opposed to mere quantity of life which finds expression more particularly in the sphere of education. It is partly because

I am a snob, partly because I honestly desire to give my children a better chance in the competitive struggle for jobs than those of my neighbour, that I prefer to send them to a fee-paying rather than to a free school. But if I am to do this, I must have not more than one or at most two children.

(6) The spiritual *malaise* of a generation that has no religion, has experienced two wars and fears a third, and has therefore a lively expectation that any children it may bring into the world will shortly assume the *rôle* of fodder for bombs and leave it.

(7) The spreading practice of birth control which enables all the other causes to become operative while at the same time preserving the pleasures of sexual intercourse which, having been invented by nature to serve as the bait on life's hook, can now be swallowed without the hook.

Children Wanted and Unwanted

It has been the argument of the preceding pages that the spread of birth control is a factor of unique importance which has promoted what is in effect a revolution in human life. This argument is fully borne out by the views expressed by the many expert writers in the book to which I have already several times referred.[1] My guess is that the great majority of all the children who have been born to all the people that have lived upon the earth have been unwanted, or if this be thought too harsh a word, unplanned. When

[1] *Rebuilding Family Life in the Post-war World.*

in the past people had children, they did not have
them because they wanted to have them; they had
them because they were the unwanted or at least un-
intended by-products of the sexual intercourse in
which the parents took their pleasure. Thus, life was
the cost of the parents' pleasure which the children
were called upon to defray.

The new factor, as I pointed out in 1924, is that the
pleasure can now be enjoyed without the children,
with the result that there is a growing tendency for
only planned and wanted children to be born. These
planned and wanted children are comparatively few.

In the report of a recent investigation of family life
by a trained psychiatric worker, Mrs. Moya Wood-
side, the expenses of which were supplied out of re-
search funds contributed by the Rockefeller Foundation, it is stated that "the families that planned to
those that did not were as five to two; and yet in the
planning families about one child in three was the
result of an accident. Taking all families together
there were more children that were accidental than
had been planned." In other words, birth control is
still far from fool-proof. As birth control technique
grows easier and more efficient, we must expect that
the number of unwanted children who are born will
grow fewer still. Finally, only wanted children will
be produced, and the birth-rate will, therefore, be
smaller than it is now.

Many of those who are optimistic in regard to the
future of the birth-rate, who hope, that is to say, and
expect that the birth-rate will rise, seem to me to

overlook the significance of the foregoing arguments. Thus, in her contribution to *Rebuilding Family Life in the Post-war World,* Dr. Margaret Jackson, writing on the *" Causes and Significance of the Dwindling Family,"* attributes the limitation of offspring to "the desire to get on in the world." We are, she points out, a highly acquisitive society and life " for many means little more than a struggle for existence on a level of tolerable material comfort."

Quite so. But when was it not so? Or when were the values which dominate society other than acquisitive? Yet throughout all the centuries of man's past, when he has had to struggle in the sweat of his brow to achieve the minimum conditions of material comfort and when the motives which guided his conduct were predominantly acquisitive, he has permitted himself to be burdened with many children. Why? Because he did not know how to prevent his wife from having them. Thus it is not because our society is acquisitive and materialistic in some sense in which previous societies have been unacquisitive and idealistic that the babies grow fewer; it is because and, in my view, almost wholly because the wish to avoid babies which has always been present is now for the first time, so far as poor people are concerned, enabled to find fulfilment.

From this point of view birth control acts like a sieve. Previously the great majority of acts of sexual intercourse resulted in children provided, of course, that conception had not already taken place. In other words, there was no sieve. Now the results of the "congress of the sexes" as the biologists so distressfully call it, are sifted; only those acts result in children which are allowed to pass through the sieve. Or, to put the point differently, throughout most of human history people have had no choice in regard to the children whom they have brought into the world. "Shall we have a child or not?" was not a question which they could effectively put to themselves, because the urgency of desire plus the propinquity of marriage produced circumstances which forced their hands. Now for the first time they have a choice; now for the first time the question can be asked and is answered for the most part in the negative. I repeat, therefore, my conclusion that, as birth control appliances become more efficient and more people resort to their use, the birth-rate will drop to a still lower level.

The Separation of Love from Parenthood

It is possible to discern any other results of the practice of birth control which, latent twenty years ago in the womb of time, when *Thrasymachus* first appeared, have since been brought to birth—I ask apology for the extreme inappropriateness of the metaphor—by twenty years' extensive and intensive use of birth control methods? I think there is one which, faintly adumbrated in the early chapters of this book, has since more clearly defined itself.

Twenty years ago it was possible to see that birth control facilitated sexual experiment. If men and women could enjoy sexual experience, nay more could establish substantial and semi-permanent sexual relationships without fear of offspring, it was obvious. that they would grasp the opportunity. They would, I thought, form all manner of relationships from the fleeting to the temporary and from the temporary to the permanent, when they were no longer hampered by the obligation to maintain children as the fruit of the relationship. I find this view endorsed by Professor Crew in the work to which I have already made reference. "It is to be expected," he writes, " that the emanicipation of women will become further enlarged and that many more alternatives to marriage and motherhood will be discovered, that divorce will be more free and that the institution of marriage will undergo further changes as the attitude of the general public towards sexual behaviour becomes modified through the replacement of ecclesiastical authority by scientific knowledge."

So much, I repeat, was sufficiently obvious. What was not, I think, so clear twenty years ago was that the general effect of sexual experimentation would be to divorce romantic love from reproductive intercourse, to separate in other words the functions of mistress and wife.

What the average male has hitherto expected of the average female in the marriage relationship has been altogether too much of a good thing. Looking at her through the spectacles of romantic love, he has expected to see and has, in fact, seen a being endowed not only with the desirability of a Venus, but with the virtues of a Madonna, the intelligence of an Athena and the talents and capacities of a first-rate housewife and, still under the influence of romantic passion, has assured himself that in comparison with the possession of the person of this epitome of all the excellences nothing in the world was of the slightest importance. This belief, that all the virtues can be found in the same woman is illusory. What is, perhaps, surprising is that society should for so long not only have tolerated but encouraged the illusion. Birth control renders further tolerance unnecessary.

The Proper Basis for Marriage

The reasons which lead a man to take a wife are various and most of them are well known. He can marry to join two pieces of land, or to mate two fortunes; he can marry because of community of religion, or because of the geographical proximity of the two families, or to please her parents or to please his, or because she knows his tastes and needs, or because both have and like the same friends, or because both want children. All these are good reasons for marriage because in respect of all of them there is a fair presumption that the weight of the considerations which lead to the marriage being contracted will persist and even increase after it has been contracted. Thus, if there was ever good reason for contracting, there will remain good reason for maintaining the marriage. Love is also a reason for marriage, but of all the reasons I have mentioned it is the worst, since in the case of love and love alone the consideration which led to the marriage being formed rarely continues long to operate after it has been formed. Love is a great and a devouring passion, a ravening beast. But when the beast has been glutted, he ceases to raven. Now you can get to the top of Mont Blanc but you cannot live there; presently you have to descend to the plains through which, a sober pedestrian, you must plod for the remaining years of your life. The most that you can hope is that the beast glutted will subside into something gracious and homely, will become in fact a domestic pet.

But though you cannot stay on Mont Blanc, you can ascend other mountains. In fact, given birth control, you can ascend quite a number of them. The moral would seem to be that provision for romantic and passionate love will now increasingly be found not within but outside the marriage relationship. The marriage relation will gain, since the reasons which led to the marriage being formed will not suddenly or gradually disappear and leave the relation hanging in the air; romantic love will gain since, no longer being burdened with irrelevant accretions, with contracts and houses and settlements and furniture and obligations and relations and children, it can burn with its pure gem-like flame for so long as there is fuel to maintain it and go out when it pleases.

These considerations are gradually beginning to colour imaginative forecasts of the family and its future from the circumspect avowal of Dr. Slater that " with an ever more universal knowledge of the technique of contraception, we have to expect that married people, as well as single, will sometimes have passing infatuations or indulge in short-lived adventures," to her considered conclusion that "society is now in a transitional stage in which the separation of sexual love and parenthood are proceeding apace. From the point of view of the happiness of the family, the health of the children, and the vigour of the race, the separation is to be welcomed on every count." With this diagnosis I am in warm agreement; the concluding sentiment I echo with a hearty cheer.

Artificial Insemination

Dr. Slater's conclusion is reinforced by a development which when this book was first published was still hidden in the future. This is the practice of artificial insemination. Artificial insemination is the impregnation of the female by the seed of the male which has been preserved by scientific processes and is then artificially introduced. It has been practised for some time past in this country in the fertilisation of cattle with a very large measure of success. (There are already six artificial insemination stations for cattle in England and Wales.) There is no medical or physiological reason why it should not be successfully practised in the case of human beings. Indeed, it has been so practised in America on a considerable scale and In this country on a small scale for some years past. I am told that one English clinic receives no less than two hundred applications a month for artificial insemination treatment. Safeguards adopted are that the women inseminated should be married and that their husbands should be sterile; that the name of the father should be withheld from the mother, but that he should be guaranteed by the clinic healthy and immune from heritable disease. Volunteers for the provision of male semen have, I understand, in certain cases been asked for and have offered themselves.

It will be seen that this process carries to its logical conclusion the separation of sexual love and parenthood. Dr. Mace, to whom I referred above, estimates that in at least 50 per cent. of childless marriages it is the male and not the female who is sterile. The value of artificial insemination to the wives of sterile husbands when both parties want children is, therefore, obvious.

But why, one wonders, should it be confined to married women? Our society is one in which the number of females considerably exceeds the number of males. After the last war the excess of females was nearly two million; even at the present time there are, according to Dr. Slater's estimate, " approximately a million women of marriageable age who could never find a husband, even if none of the men remained single."

Our present system presents these women with the alternatives either of frustrating the instinct of motherhood or of exercising it at the cost of social ostracism for themselves and illegitimacy for their children. This seems to me cruel and unjust.

The Three Sexual Freedoms

The argument of the foregoing book pleaded for three sexual freedoms, first, the freedom not to be forced to bring into the world unwanted children. This entails the approval of birth control and with certain safeguards of the practice of abortion. Secondly, the freedom not to be forced to live with somebody, who is distasteful to one. This entails making divorce easy, cheap and honourable. Thirdly, the freedom for women who want children to have them without being saddled with the obligation to live with, mother and make a fuss of a man.

Of these freedoms, all of which still seem to me to be desirable, it is the third which is facilitated by artificial insemination. I do not know how to put the case for it better than it has been put by Miss Mary O'Brien of Pacific Highway, Chatswood, a fashionable suburb of Sydney, who in a letter to the Press in May, 1945, endorsed the suggestion of the President of the Western Australia Women's Service Guild that unmarried women who desired artificially inseminated children should be permitted to avail themselves of this method.

" I am," she writes, " a lonely unwanted spinster. My fiancé was killed in the first World War. I longed for a baby more than anything else in life. What does society permit me to have? A parrot and a cat. Laugh—yes, laugh. Married women with families jeer and ridicule my attachment to these poor substitutes for children's loving arms. I was a girl with natural maternal instincts; but what have I now? An empty heart and a soured temperament, all because a right was denied me. If a girl single or married wants to fulfil her natural function, let her have a child, and let us admire her desire for motherhood, not slander and ostracise her. People will say, 'What of the laws?' I say, 'Alter them.'"

The argument is simple and in my view cogent. It is that an unmarried mother devoted to her child is likely to be a better and certainly a happier citizen than a frustrated spinster or a deliberately childless matron. As there is no suggestion of sexual pleasure in the process of artificial insemination, one might have supposed that the puritanical voices of the jealous and the envious would have been stilled. This, however, is not the case. The process is new and the effects upon society of its adoption are difficult to gauge. Moreover, it is clear that it strikes a fresh blow at the family. It is no surprise, then, to learn that as a preliminary measure, thinking no doubt that it is well to be on the safe side, the Ministry of Health has ruled that all births resulting from artificial insemination should be registered as illegitimate.

The Argument About the Soul

There are also, I gather from a recent weighty debate in the House of Lords, theological objections touching the immortal soul of the artificially inseminated child.

I cannot, I am afraid, see the difficulty. Either you are a materialist, in which case you think that the universe consists of matter and that there exists no immaterial or spiritual element in the world in addition to the material particles of which it is composed. If this is your view, then it follows that we are all body and only body. Provided, then, that the body is healthy, is normal and functions normally, the precise method by which it came into existence is surely, for you, a matter of unimportance.

Or you may think, as I do, that in addition to the stuff of which our bodies are made, we contain, or, if you prefer it put that way, our essence consists in being a spiritual activity. Of this activity our bodies are the vehicles. It has been usual to denominate this activity " the soul "; in modern times it is called non-committally " the mind." The soul or mind, on this view, animates our bodies, directs the matter of which they are formed and in all probability survives them. How this immaterial element " gets into " the body, if I may permit myself to use a spatial metaphor, is and always has been a mystery. Lucretius in the *De Rerum Natura,* writing as a convinced materialist, makes great play with the notion of a string of disembodied souls queueing up outside in the passage, whenever sexual intercourse occurs, in the hope of being the first to gain entry into and take possession of the impregnated ovum. The caricature receives a certain plausibility from the ignorance which disables us from demonstrating its falsehood. We know in a general sort of way that things don't happen like that, but how precisely they do happen we do not know. The creation of a personality is in fact a mystery.

But precisely because we do not believe that a "something" enters into the impregnated ovum which is other than the matter of which the ovum is composed, we find it difficult to regard the matter of the ovum as relevant to the issue. If, in fact, you believe in the importance of the soul, you must also believe in the comparative unimportance of the body. The body is merely the vehicle in which the soul travels, the garment which it wears during its temporary sojourn on the earth. Quite so; but if so, why attribute this overwhelming significance to the precise method by which the body is formed? I would not go so far as to say that one method is as good as another. The natural way no doubt is the better; it is certainly the more pleasurable; but where for any reason the natural method is impracticable, why should we object to the formation of bodies by some other method? After all, there are still the sperm and the ovum; there are still two parents and the artificially inseminated child comes into the world with the regulation stock of genes and chromosomes by means of which such characteristics of the parents as are heritable are conveyed to it.

Suppose that we agree that the child is more than the sum total of its physiological inheritance, that it is in fact that mysterious thing a living personality; that this personality is immaterial and is not therefore identical with or resolvable into the body; and that if any part of it survives death, it is this, the im-

138

material part, that does so. Let us also agree that the personality is not *wholly* derived from the parents. If we do agree to these propositions, with what logic do we prevent women who are starved of motherhood from exercising their natural function, on the score of what is after all only a point of mechanistic pedantry? It is the wares that a man brings to market that concern us, not the vehicle in which they are conveyed. Finally, if we are concerned about the decline of the birth-rate and really want more children, why should we look down our noses at this new and unexpected source of supply? For my part, I would welcome a decline in the birth-rate and would like to see a very much smaller population in this country. But that is another story, and a long one.